RELATIONSHIP HACKS

AMANDA LAMBROS

ISBN: 978-1-923237-00-1

DEDICATION

To my parents, for their boundless love and unwavering belief in me.

To my husband, my steadfast partner, whose support, patience, and encouragement continue to remind me what a strong partnership looks like.

To my sons, who bring light, laughter, and perspective into my life every day, and who keep me grounded in what truly matters.

And to the relationship therapists, mentors, and educators whose wisdom and dedication have helped shape my understanding of the beauty and complexity of human connection.

This book exists because of all of you.

First published in 2026 by Amanda Lambros

Growth Mindset Publications
PO Box 226 Victoria Park WA 6979
www.growthmindsetpublications.com

A catalogue entry for this book is available from the National Library of Australia.

Paperback: 978-1-923237-00-1

Printed in Australia
Project management and text design by Roselyn Castrodes
Cover design by Peter L., 52 Design Studio
Author Photo by Kat Wray, Red Eclectic

The paper this book is printed on is certified as environmentally friendly.

Disclaimer

ACKNOWLEDGMENTS

This book would not have been possible without the unwavering love and support of several remarkable individuals in my life.

First and foremost, I am deeply grateful to my parents, whose endless encouragement and belief in me have been the cornerstone of my journey. Their love has provided me with the strength and inspiration to pursue my dreams every step of the way. Mom, you have been my greatest cheerleader, and for that, I am eternally thankful.

To my hubby... your patience and understanding for everything and anything that I put my mind is palpable. Thanks for always being there no matter what. Our journey together has taught me so much about the complexities and beauty of relationships and I wouldn’t trade it for the world.

To my young men, you make my heart feel full. Watching you grow has enriched my understanding of human connections and deepened my appreciation for the bonds we share. I love embarking on new experiences with you both.

I also wish to extend my heartfelt gratitude to all the relationship therapists and mentors who have come before me. Your wisdom, guidance, and dedication to the field have paved the way for my work. Your contributions have not only influenced my own professional growth but have also helped countless individuals navigate the intricate dynamics of their relationships.

Thank you all for your love, support, and invaluable contributions to my life and work. This book is a testament to the power of relationships and the profound impact they have on our lives.

TABLE OF CONTENTS

1: Foundations of Healthy Relationships

2: Strengthening Connection

3: Navigating Conflict and Repair

4: Growing Together

5: Creating a Life Together

“Healthy relationships aren’t built through grand gestures. They are built through small, consistent choices to care for each other every day.”

- AMANDA LAMBROS

Author's Note

Relationships are one of the most important parts of our lives.

They shape how we experience joy, how we navigate challenges, and how supported we feel as we move through the world. Yet despite their importance, very few of us are ever formally taught how to build and maintain healthy relationships.

Over the past two decades, I've had the privilege of working with thousands of individuals and couples navigating the complexities of love, communication, and partnership. Through those experiences, one thing has become incredibly clear to me.

Strong relationships are not built by chance.

They are built through small, intentional actions practiced consistently over time.

The ideas in this book come from years of professional experience, conversations with couples, and the patterns I have observed in relationships that thrive as well as those that struggle.

My hope is that the strategies and reflections in these pages help you strengthen your connection, improve communication, and build a relationship that continues to grow and evolve.

Whether you read this book on your own, discuss it with your partner, or return to it occasionally for inspiration, I encourage you to approach it with curiosity and openness.

Relationships are not about perfection.

They are about two people learning, growing, and choosing each other again and again.

Thank you for taking the time to invest in your relationship.

Warmly,
Amanda Lambros

A Story from the Therapy Room

A couple once sat across from me in my office, both looking equally frustrated.

They had been together for more than ten years.

From the outside, their life looked stable. They had built a home together, shared responsibilities, and genuinely cared about each other. But in that moment, they felt completely disconnected.

"I don't understand how we got here," the wife said.

"We used to be so close."

Her partner nodded quietly before adding, "It feels like we're just managing life together now. Not really connecting."

As we talked, something became very clear.

They still loved each other deeply.

What they didn't have were the **skills and habits required to maintain a strong relationship over time**.

Over the years they had slowly stopped doing many of the small things that once made them feel connected.

They stopped asking curious questions about each other's day.
They stopped expressing appreciation regularly.
They stopped prioritising time together.

Not because they didn't care.

But because life became busy and the relationship slowly moved to the background.

This pattern is far more common than people realise.

Most couples don't suddenly fall out of love.

More often, they gradually drift apart when the daily habits that strengthen connection begin to disappear.

The encouraging part of this story is what happened next.

Once this couple began learning a few simple relationship skills, things started to shift.

They began listening to each other differently.
They started having small, intentional conversations again.
They brought back moments of appreciation and connection that had quietly disappeared.

Slowly, their relationship began to feel lighter.

More connected.
More supportive.
More like the partnership they remembered building together years earlier.

Experiences like this are exactly why this book exists.

Over the past two decades, I've worked with thousands of couples navigating the complexities of relationships. And one thing has become very clear:

Healthy relationships are not built by accident.

They are built through small, intentional habits practiced consistently over time.

Inside this book you'll find 100 practical relationship hacks designed to help you strengthen communication, deepen connection, and invest in the relationship you want to build together.

Some will feel simple.

Some might challenge the way you currently approach things.

All of them are designed to help you reconnect with what matters most.

Because strong relationships are not about perfection.

They are about two people who keep choosing to learn, grow, and show up for each other.

Introduction

Ask and you shall receive.

After working with thousands of couples over the past few decades, one request has come up again and again.

"Do you have a book with practical tips we can use between sessions?"

So, here it is.

Before we go any further, let me say something important.

This book is not a replacement for working with a therapist you trust and feel safe being completely open with. In fact, I strongly believe that when couples are facing significant challenges, professional support can be incredibly valuable.

However, what many couples need in between those sessions is something practical. A reminder. A small nudge. A tool they can return to when everyday life gets busy.

That's exactly what this book is designed to be.

Think of it as a practical companion that keeps your relationship at the forefront of your mind.

Because relationships don't strengthen by accident. They strengthen when we intentionally invest in them.

In today's world, relationships are navigating a complex landscape. We are more connected through technology than ever before, yet many people feel emotionally disconnected from the people closest to them.

Couples often find themselves juggling careers, responsibilities, stress, and endless distractions, all while trying to maintain meaningful connection with their partner.

It's no surprise that many people feel uncertain about how to navigate the challenges that arise.

Relationships are at the core of the human experience. They shape our happiness, influence our wellbeing, and play a significant role in how we experience life.

Yet despite their importance, very few of us are ever taught the skills required to build and maintain strong relationships.

Communication.
Conflict resolution.
Emotional connection.
Trust.

These are all skills that can be learned and strengthened over time.

This book brings together insights drawn from years of professional experience, personal observation, and evidence-based relationship research.

Inside these pages you will find **100 practical relationship hacks** designed to help you:

• communicate more effectively
• strengthen trust and emotional connection
• navigate conflict in healthier ways
• support each other's personal growth
• build a relationship that continues to evolve over time

Each hack offers a simple strategy you can apply in everyday life. Some will take only a few minutes to implement, while others may inspire deeper reflection and conversation.

The goal is not perfection.

The goal is progress.

Because strong relationships are built through small actions practiced consistently.

My hope is that this book becomes something you return to again and again. A reminder that relationships deserve attention, care, and investment.

Thank you for taking the time to invest in your relationship.

Let's begin.

The Three Biggest Relationship Mistakes I See Every Day

After more than two decades of working with couples, I can tell you something with complete confidence.

Most relationships don't fail because people stop loving each other.

They struggle because people stop **investing in the relationship in the right ways**.

Over the years I have worked with thousands of couples. Different ages. Different backgrounds. Different relationship stories.

And yet, I see the same three patterns appear again and again.

If you recognise yourself in any of these, don't worry. You're not alone. In fact, you're human.

The good news is that once you recognise these patterns, you can start changing them.

Mistake #1

Expecting Your Partner to Read Your Mind

One of the most common frustrations I hear from couples sounds something like this:

"If they really loved me, they would just know."

Know what you need.
Know what you're feeling.
Know what upset you.

But here's the tough truth.

Your partner is not a mind reader.

Healthy relationships are built on communication, not silent expectations.

When needs go unspoken, disappointment grows. Over time that disappointment can turn into resentment.

The couples who build strong relationships are the ones who learn how to say things like:

- "I need more support with this."
- "That really hurt my feelings."
- "Can we talk about something that's been on my mind?"

Clear communication isn't unromantic.

It's responsible.

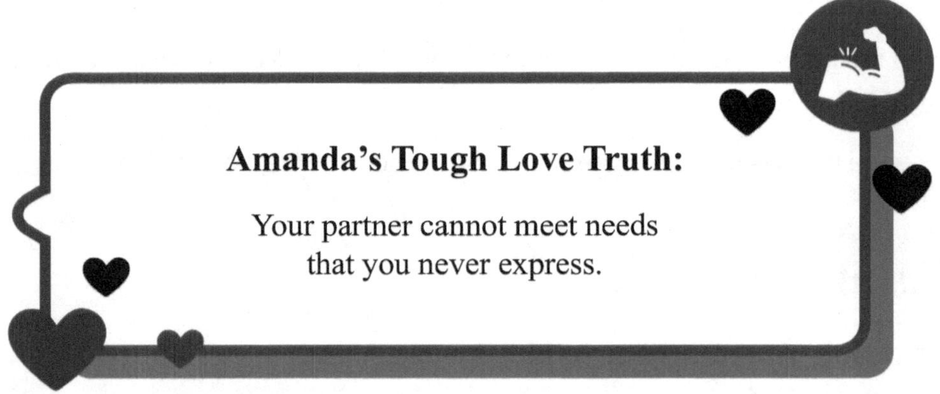

Mistake #2

Stopping the Small Relationship Habits

At the beginning of a relationship, couples tend to do the little things naturally.

They ask about each other's day.
They say thank you.

They show affection.
They make time for each other.

Then life gets busy.

Work. Kids. Responsibilities. Stress.

And those small habits slowly disappear.

Here's what many people don't realise.

Research from relationship psychologist Dr John Gottman shows that strong relationships are not built on grand romantic gestures.

They are built on **small daily moments of connection**.

A kind word.
A quick hug.
A moment of attention.

When those moments disappear, emotional distance starts to grow.

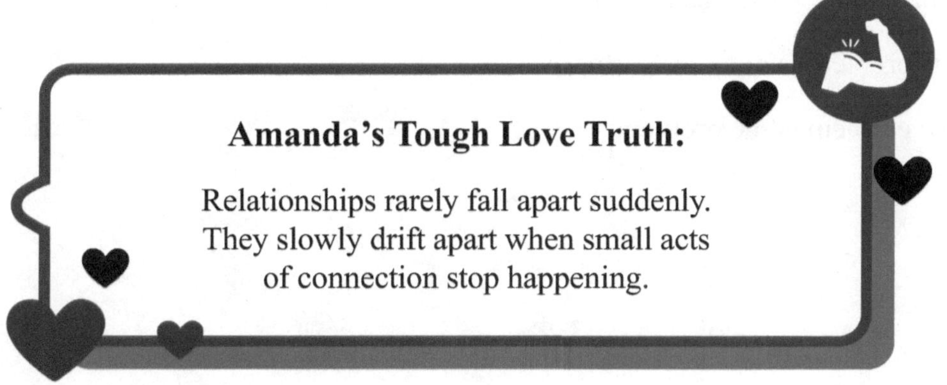

Mistake #3

Treating Your Partner Like the Problem Instead of the Teammate

Conflict is normal in every relationship.

Two different people will naturally have different perspectives.

But when couples begin treating each other like opponents instead of teammates, everything changes.

Instead of solving the problem together, the focus becomes:

• Who's right
• Who's wrong
• Who's to blame

That mindset turns small disagreements into emotional battles.

Healthy couples approach conflict differently.

They shift the conversation from:

"You did this."

to

"How do we solve this together?"

The problem is not your partner.

The problem is the problem.

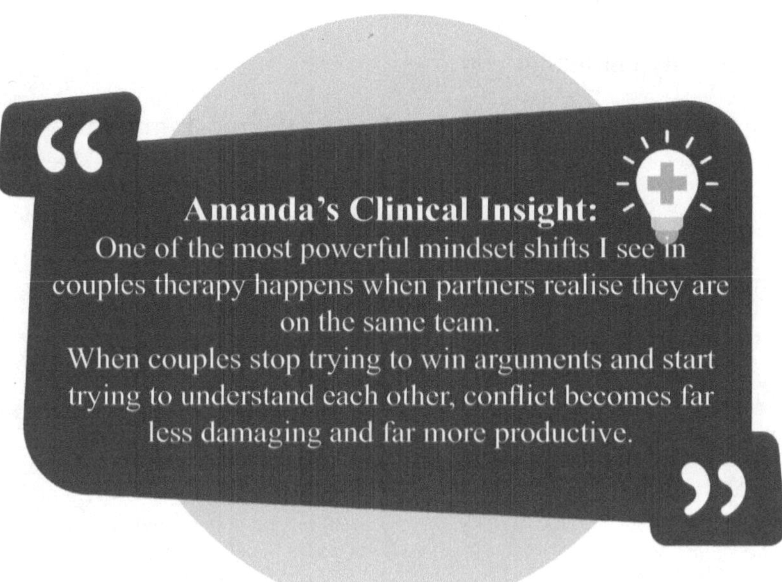

The Good News

If any of these mistakes feel familiar, you're not alone.

Most couples were never taught the skills required to build strong relationships.

We learn maths in school.

We learn science.

But very few people are taught how to communicate, resolve conflict, or maintain emotional connection in a relationship.

That's exactly why this book exists.

Inside the following pages you'll find **100 practical relationship hacks** designed to help you strengthen your connection, improve communication, and build a healthier partnership.

Some of them are simple.

Some of them may challenge you.

All of them are designed to help you invest in the most important relationship in your life.

Let's begin.

How to Use This Book

This book is designed to be practical.

Not theoretical.
Not complicated.
Not something you read once and then place on a shelf.

Each relationship hack in this book is a small, actionable strategy that can help strengthen your connection, improve communication, and build a healthier partnership over time.

You don't need to read the book in one sitting (although you absolutely can if that's your style). Instead, think of this book as a toolkit you can return to again and again.

Some couples like to read a few hacks together each week and discuss them. Others prefer to reflect on them individually and bring the insights into their conversations.

There is no "right" way to use this book.

However, here are a few suggestions that can help you get the most out of it.

Try One Hack at a Time

You don't need to implement all one hundred hacks at once.

In fact, trying to change everything overnight rarely works.

Instead, choose one or two hacks that resonate with you and focus on applying those consistently. Small changes practiced regularly often create the biggest impact in relationships.

Use the Reflection Questions

Throughout the book you'll find reflection questions designed to help you pause and think more deeply about your relationship.

These questions are not tests. They are opportunities for insight.

You may choose to reflect on them privately, journal about them, or discuss them with your partner. Often the most meaningful conversations begin with a simple question.

Try the Micro Actions

Many of the hacks include small "micro actions" you can try immediately.

These actions are intentionally simple.

Relationships are strengthened through consistent everyday behaviour, not occasional grand gestures. The small things we do regularly often make the biggest difference.

Be Curious, Not Defensive

Some of the ideas in this book may challenge the way you currently approach certain situations in your relationship.

That's normal.

The goal is not to blame yourself or your partner, but to become more aware of patterns that may not be serving your relationship as well as they could.

Approach the process with curiosity rather than criticism.

Growth always begins with awareness.

Progress, Not Perfection

No relationship is perfect.

Every couple experiences misunderstandings, disagreements, and difficult periods. What matters most is the willingness to learn, grow, and keep investing in the relationship.

If even a handful of these hacks help you improve communication, strengthen connection, or better understand your partner, then this book will have done its job.

Relationships thrive when both people continue choosing each other.

And sometimes the smallest changes can make the biggest difference.

The Relationship Investment Principle

Most people understand the concept of financial investment.

If you want your money to grow, you invest consistently over time. Small, regular deposits eventually create significant returns.

Relationships work in much the same way.

Healthy relationships don't thrive by accident. They grow when both people consistently invest time, attention, effort, and care into the partnership.

I like to call this **The Relationship Investment Principle**.

Every positive action you take in your relationship acts like a deposit into an emotional bank account.

A thoughtful message.
A moment of genuine listening.
A hug when your partner has had a difficult day.
Saying thank you for something that might otherwise go unnoticed.

Each of these moments strengthens the emotional connection between two people.

Over time, these small deposits build trust, security, and resilience within the relationship.

On the other hand, when couples stop investing in their relationship, emotional withdrawals begin to occur.

Criticism.
Disconnection.
Neglect.
Unspoken resentment.

Without enough positive deposits to balance those withdrawals, the relationship begins to feel strained.

Research from relationship psychologist Dr John Gottman highlights the importance of maintaining a strong balance of positive interactions in relationships. In fact, his studies suggest that thriving couples experience significantly more positive interactions than negative ones.

The good news is that relationship investment does not require grand gestures.

The most powerful investments are often the smallest ones.

The hacks throughout this book are designed to help you make **consistent, meaningful deposits into your relationship**.

Because when both partners keep investing, the returns can be extraordinary.

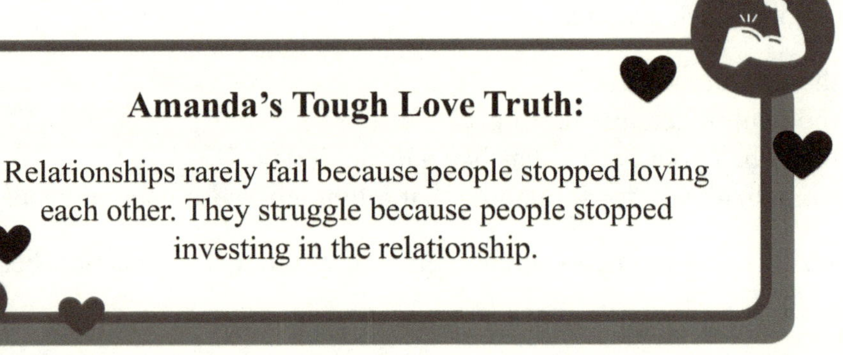

A Simple Question to Consider

If your relationship were a bank account, would you say you are currently making more deposits or withdrawals?

What Healthy Couples Do Differently

After working with thousands of individuals and couples over the past two decades, I've noticed something very interesting.

Healthy relationships are not necessarily the ones with the fewest challenges.

They are the ones where both partners have learned the skills to navigate those challenges together.

Thriving couples are not perfect. They argue, misunderstand each other, and occasionally get things wrong just like everyone else.

The difference is that they consistently practice a handful of behaviours that strengthen their relationship over time.

Here are five things I see healthy couples doing differently.

1. They Stay Curious About Each Other

One of the most common patterns I see in struggling relationships is that couples slowly stop asking questions about each other.

Early in a relationship, curiosity is natural.

You want to know everything about the other person. Their dreams, their opinions, their experiences, and the small details that make them who they are.

Over time, that curiosity can quietly fade. Conversations become focused on logistics rather than connection.

Healthy couples remain curious about each other, even years into the relationship.

They continue asking questions, exploring new interests together, and learning about how their partner is evolving.

People grow and change over time. Curious partners grow with them.

Amanda's Tough Love Truth:

If you think you already know everything about your partner, you've probably stopped paying attention.

2. They Address Problems Early

Every relationship experiences tension at times.

But thriving couples tend to address issues while they are still small rather than allowing frustration to quietly build.

When concerns are ignored, resentment often grows beneath the surface. Eventually, something relatively minor can trigger a much larger argument because it represents months or even years of unspoken frustration.

Healthy couples practice early conversations. They are willing to say things like:

"Something has been on my mind that I'd like us to talk about."

Addressing issues early prevents emotional distance from developing.

3. They Prioritise Connection

Life becomes busy.

Careers, responsibilities, children, finances, and everyday pressures can quickly fill every available moment.

In the midst of all of this, thriving couples make a conscious effort to protect their connection.

They create small rituals that keep them emotionally close.

Morning coffee together.
A regular walk.
A weekly date night.
A quick check-in at the end of the day.

These small moments signal something very important:

"Our relationship matters."

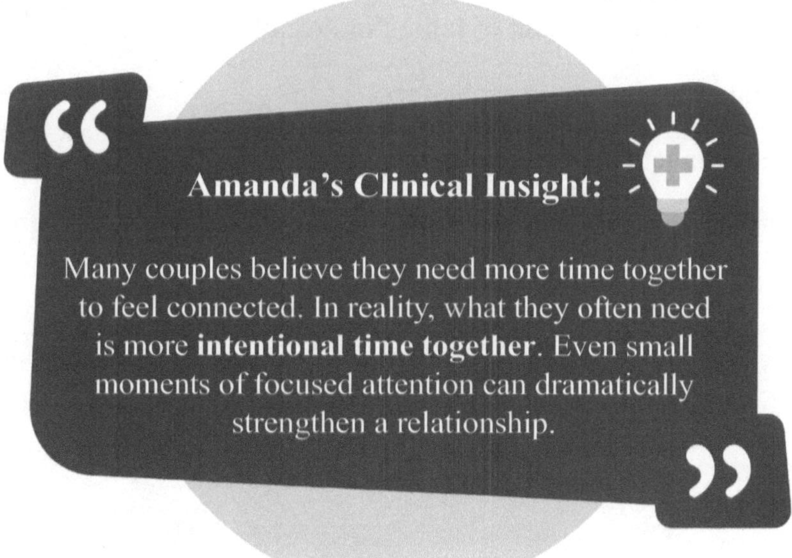

4. They Work as a Team

One of the healthiest mindset shifts in relationships is moving from **“me versus you”** to **“us versus the problem.”**

When couples start seeing each other as opponents, conflict becomes a battle.

When they see themselves as teammates, conflict becomes something they solve together.

Healthy couples understand that they are on the same side.

Even when they disagree.

5. They Keep Investing in the Relationship

Strong relationships don’t run on autopilot.

They require attention, effort, and care over time.

The couples who thrive are the ones who continue investing in their relationship long after the early excitement of falling in love has settled.

They continue learning about each other.

They continue practicing healthy communication.

They continue making deposits into the emotional bank account of the relationship.

And that is exactly what the strategies in this book are designed to help you do.

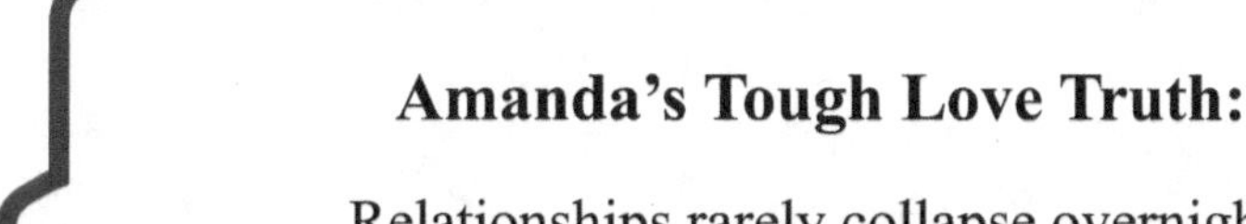

Amanda's Tough Love Truth:

Relationships rarely collapse overnight. More often, they slowly weaken when couples stop investing in them.

Ready to Start?

The hacks in the following pages are simple but powerful strategies designed to help you strengthen your connection, improve communication, and build a relationship that continues to grow over time.

You don't need to implement all of them at once.

Just start with one.

Small changes practiced consistently can create remarkable results.

Let's begin.

Amanda's 10 Relationship Rules

Over the years I've had the privilege of working with thousands of individuals and couples navigating the joys and challenges of relationships.

Some relationships are new and exciting. Others have been together for decades. Some couples arrive feeling deeply connected, while others arrive wondering how things became so difficult.

Despite the different circumstances, I've noticed something fascinating.

Healthy relationships tend to follow a similar set of guiding principles.

These principles are not complicated, but they do require intention and consistency. When couples apply them regularly, relationships become stronger, more resilient, and far more enjoyable.

I like to think of these as **The 10 Relationship Rules**.

Rule 1

You Are Teammates, Not Opponents

Your partner is not the enemy.

Even during disagreements, the goal should always be to solve the problem together rather than win the argument.

Healthy couples move from **"you versus me"** to **"us versus the problem."**

Rule 2

Communication Beats Assumption

Mind reading is not a relationship skill.

If something matters to you, express it clearly and respectfully. Healthy communication reduces misunderstanding and builds trust.

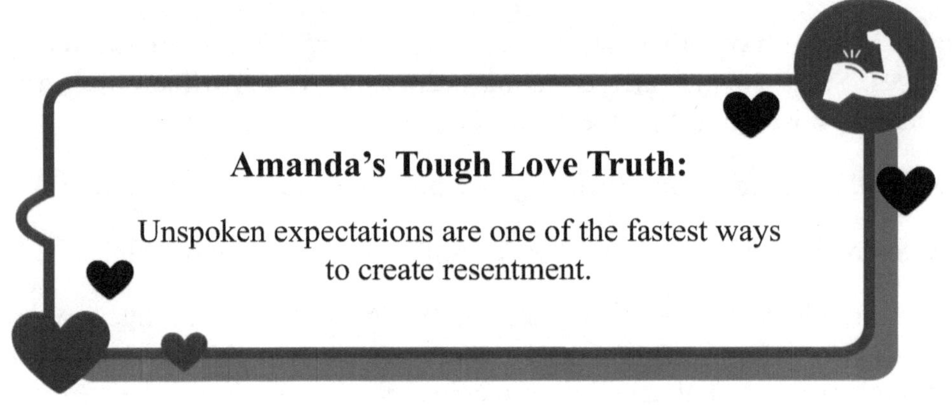

Rule 3

Small Moments Matter More Than Grand Gestures

Relationships are strengthened by everyday actions.

A kind word.
A hug.
A moment of attention.

Over time, these small moments create deep emotional connection.

Rule 4

Appreciation Should Be Expressed Regularly

Feeling valued is one of the most powerful emotional experiences in a relationship.

Don't assume your partner knows you appreciate them. Tell them.

Often.

Rule 5

Conflict Is Normal. Disrespect Is Not

Every couple disagrees.

What matters is how those disagreements are handled.

Healthy couples focus on understanding rather than attacking.

Rule 6

Growth Is Good for Relationships

Strong relationships encourage individual growth.

When both partners continue developing emotionally, intellectually, and personally, the relationship evolves alongside them.

Rule 7

Protect the Connection

Life will always present distractions.

Work, responsibilities, stress, and technology can easily consume our attention.

Healthy couples intentionally protect time for connection.

Rule 8

Curiosity Keeps Relationships Alive

The person you fell in love with years ago is not exactly the same person today.

People grow and change.

Healthy couples stay curious about who their partner is becoming.

Rule 9

Emotional Safety Is Essential

Your partner should feel safe expressing their thoughts and feelings with you.

When people feel emotionally safe, trust deepens and communication improves.

Rule 10

Keep Choosing Each Other

Long-term relationships are not sustained by love alone.

They are sustained by repeated choices to show up, invest, support, and care for one another.

Healthy relationships are built one intentional choice at a time.

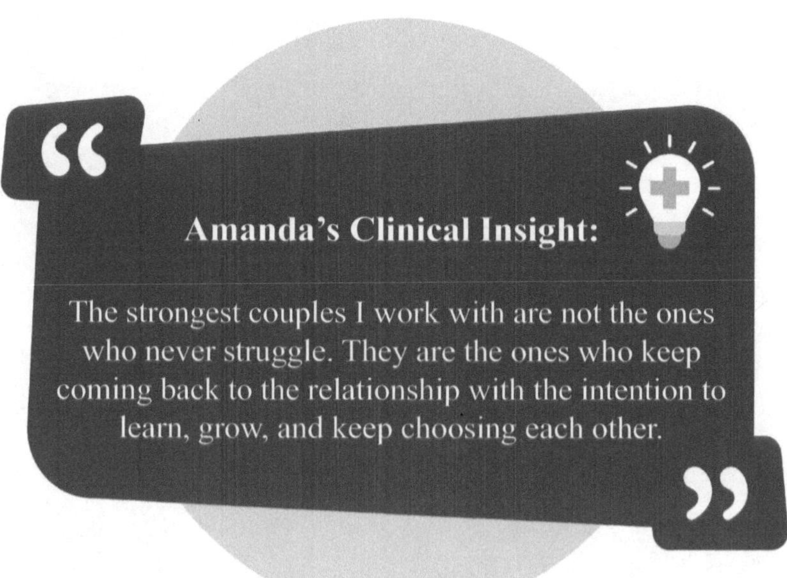

A Final Thought

The hacks throughout this book are designed to help you put these rules into practice.

You don't need to master them all immediately.

Just start with one.

Small actions practiced consistently can transform the way you experience your relationship.

SECTION ONE: FOUNDATIONS OF HEALTHY RELATIONSHIPS

"Great relationships are not built on luck. They are built on skills that anyone can learn and practice."

Why This Section Matters

Every strong relationship begins with a solid foundation.

Without the basic skills of communication, respect, and emotional awareness, even the most loving partnerships can struggle. Many couples assume that love alone should be enough to sustain a relationship, but the reality is that love needs the support of healthy habits and practical skills.

Unfortunately, most of us were never formally taught how to build strong relationships. We learned about relationships by observing others, often absorbing patterns from family, culture, or past experiences. Some of those patterns serve us well, while others can quietly create misunderstandings and frustration.

The hacks in this section focus on the essential skills that form the backbone of healthy relationships. These skills help partners communicate clearly, understand each other's needs, and create an environment where both people feel respected and valued.

When these foundations are strong, the rest of the relationship has room to grow.

Amanda's Tough Love Truth:

Love might bring two people together, but skills are what keep them together.

Hack 1
Listen Actively

Have you ever shared something important with your partner only to realise halfway through that they're not really listening?

They're nodding. Maybe even saying "uh-huh." But their eyes keep drifting to their phone or the television. In that moment, it can feel surprisingly lonely.

In my work as a relationship therapist, one of the most common complaints I hear from couples is this:
"I just don't feel heard."

Active listening is one of the most powerful relationship skills you can develop. It means giving your partner your full attention, not just hearing their words but genuinely trying to understand their experience.

Research from the Gottman Institute shows that couples who respond positively to each other's attempts to connect, known as "bids for connection," have significantly stronger relationships over time.

Active listening involves more than silence. It includes eye contact, curiosity, and occasionally reflecting back what you've heard.

When someone feels truly heard, something remarkable happens. Defensiveness drops. Emotional safety increases. And real connection begins.

The next time your partner starts sharing something about their day, pause what you're doing. Put your phone down. Face them. Listen without interrupting for at least one full minute.

Then respond with something simple like:
"I can see why that mattered to you."

When was the last time your partner genuinely felt heard by you?

Hack 2
Communicate Openly

Healthy relationships are not built on mind-reading. They are built on communication.

Yet many couples quietly expect their partner to magically understand what they are feeling without ever saying it out loud. When that doesn't happen, resentment starts to grow.

Open communication means expressing your thoughts, feelings, needs, and expectations clearly and respectfully. It also means being willing to hear your partner's perspective without immediately jumping into defence mode.

In my clinical work, I often see couples who love each other deeply but struggle because they have never learned how to communicate openly about difficult topics.

Research in relationship psychology consistently shows that couples who discuss their emotions openly report greater relationship satisfaction and emotional intimacy.

Open communication isn't always comfortable, but it is always necessary.

Tonight, ask your partner one simple question: "What's something on your mind lately that we haven't talked about?"

Then listen without interrupting.

Is there something important you've been hoping your partner would notice without you saying it?

Hack 3
Practice Empathy

Empathy is the ability to step into your partner's emotional world and see things from their perspective.

It doesn't mean you always agree with them. It simply means you make the effort to understand their experience.

One of the most common mistakes couples make during disagreements is trying to prove their point instead of trying to understand their partner.

But relationships are not courtrooms. Nobody wins when someone else loses.

Empathy changes the dynamic entirely. Instead of arguing about who is right, you begin exploring what each person is feeling.

Neuroscience research shows that when someone feels understood, their brain's threat response decreases. In simple terms, empathy calms the nervous system.

And calm people communicate much better than defensive ones.

The next time your partner is upset, resist the urge to immediately fix the problem.

Instead say:
"Help me understand what this feels like for you."

When your partner is upset, do you tend to fix the problem or understand the emotion?

Hack 4
Respect Differences

Here is one of the most important truths about relationships:

You and your partner are two completely different humans.

Different backgrounds.
Different personalities.
Different emotional triggers.
Different ways of doing life.

And that is not a problem. That is the whole point.

Many couples struggle because they unconsciously believe their partner should think the same way they do. When that doesn't happen, frustration appears.

Healthy relationships don't erase differences. They respect them.

Research in long-term relationship studies shows that many successful couples still disagree on numerous topics. What makes them successful is how they navigate those differences.

Respect means allowing space for different opinions without turning every disagreement into a battle.

The next time you and your partner disagree about something, pause and say:

"We don't have to think the same way to respect each other."

Do you try to understand your partner's perspective, or convince them that yours is correct?

Hack 5
Cultivate Trust

A relationship without trust is exhausting.

You second-guess conversations.
You question intentions.
You wonder what's really happening.

Trust removes that constant emotional tension.

Trust is built through three simple but powerful behaviours: reliability, consistency, and honesty.

When you say you will do something, do it.
When you promise something, follow through.
When something is wrong, talk about it.

Trust is not built through grand gestures. It is built through everyday reliability.

Research shows that trust in relationships grows through repeated experiences of dependability. In other words, small consistent actions matter far more than occasional big ones.

Think of one small promise you can make to your partner this week and follow through on it completely.

If your partner described you as trustworthy, what behaviours would they point to?

Hack 6
Be Present

We live in a world where people are constantly connected to devices and increasingly disconnected from each other.

You've probably experienced it before. You're talking, and the other person is scrolling.

Even if they're physically beside you, emotionally they're somewhere else.

Being present means giving your partner your attention in the moment. No phones. No multitasking. No half-listening.

Psychological studies show that couples who spend even small amounts of focused time together report stronger emotional connection than couples who spend more time together while distracted.

Quality presence beats distracted proximity every time.

Choose one moment each day where both of you put your phones away and talk for ten uninterrupted minutes.

When your partner talks to you, are you fully there?

Hack 7
Share Your Feelings

Many people grow up learning that emotions should be managed privately.

But relationships thrive on emotional openness.

Sharing how you feel allows your partner to understand what is happening inside your world. Without that insight, they are left guessing.

Emotional expression strengthens intimacy. It signals trust and vulnerability.

Studies in emotional psychology show that couples who regularly share their feelings develop stronger emotional bonds and greater resilience during stressful times.

Sharing feelings does not mean emotional dumping. It means expressing your experience honestly and respectfully.

Complete this sentence with your partner today:
"Something I've been feeling lately is…"

Are there feelings you regularly keep to yourself instead of sharing with your partner?

Hack 8
Respect Personal Boundaries

Let's be clear about something that many couples misunderstand.

Boundaries are not barriers. They are guidelines for how we treat each other with respect.

A boundary simply says: "This is what I need in order to feel safe, respected, and emotionally healthy."

Healthy relationships require two things to exist at the same time: **connection and individuality**. When boundaries are ignored, resentment quietly begins to grow.

Research in relationship psychology shows that individuals who feel their personal boundaries are respected experience higher relationship satisfaction and lower emotional burnout.

Respecting boundaries means listening when your partner communicates their limits, whether that relates to time, privacy, emotional space, friendships, or digital habits.

A relationship thrives when both people feel they can be themselves without constantly feeling pressured, controlled, or criticised.

Ask your partner this question:
"Is there anything you need more space around that we haven't talked about yet?"

Listen with curiosity, not defensiveness.

Do you see your partner's boundaries as rejection, or as a healthy part of maintaining a balanced relationship?

Hack 9
Practice Active Gratitude

Gratitude is one of the most underrated relationship skills.

When couples first fall in love, appreciation flows naturally. Over time, familiarity creeps in and many people begin focusing more on what is missing rather than what is working.

The problem is simple: what we focus on grows.

Research from positive psychology shows that couples who regularly express appreciation experience stronger emotional connection and higher long-term satisfaction in their relationships.

Gratitude doesn't require grand gestures. Often it's the small acknowledgements that make the biggest difference.

A simple "Thank you for doing that" or "I really appreciate how you handled that situation" can completely change the emotional tone of a relationship.

Today, tell your partner **one thing you genuinely appreciate about them** that you may have taken for granted.

What are three things your partner does regularly that you rarely acknowledge?

Hack 10
Prioritise Quality Time

Being in the same room is not the same as spending time together.

Many couples sit side by side every evening while staring at separate screens. Technically they are together, but emotionally they're miles apart.

Quality time is about intentional connection.

It means putting distractions aside and being genuinely present with each other. Even short periods of focused attention can strengthen emotional bonds.

According to relationship research, couples who spend consistent quality time together report greater relationship stability and emotional closeness.

The secret is not the amount of time. It's the **quality of attention**.

Choose one small ritual this week:

- a walk together
- morning coffee together
- a phone-free dinner

Protect that time like it matters, because it does.

When was the last time you and your partner spent uninterrupted time together?

Hack 11
Show Physical Affection

Human beings are wired for connection, and physical touch plays a powerful role in relationships.

Simple gestures like holding hands, hugging, or a reassuring touch on the arm communicate warmth, comfort, and closeness.

Physical affection releases oxytocin, often called the "bonding hormone," which helps reduce stress and increase feelings of connection.

Research in neuroscience shows that couples who maintain regular physical affection often report stronger emotional bonds and greater relationship satisfaction.

Touch communicates what words sometimes cannot.

Offer your partner a **20-second hug** today.

Longer hugs increase oxytocin and calm the nervous system for both people.

Has physical affection increased or decreased in your relationship over time?

Hack 12
Initiate Regular Relationship Check-ins

Most couples regularly check their bank accounts, their calendars, and their emails.

But they rarely check the health of their relationship.

That's a mistake.

Relationships need **intentional maintenance**.

One of the most effective strategies I use with couples in my practice is something I call the **Traffic Light Check-In**.

Here's how it works:

- **Red:** behaviours that need to stop
- **Yellow:** behaviours that need adjusting
- **Green:** behaviours that are working well and should continue

This creates a structured conversation where both partners can speak honestly without waiting until frustration explodes.

Schedule a weekly 20-minute relationship check-in.

Ask each other:
"What's one green, one yellow, and one red from this week?"

When was the last time you intentionally reviewed the health of your relationship?

Hack 13
Be a Good Teammate

Healthy relationships operate with a simple but powerful mindset shift.

From **“me” to “we.”**

Instead of seeing problems as something one person caused, strong couples treat challenges as something they solve together.

You’re not opponents. You’re teammates.

Research on relationship resilience shows that couples who approach conflict with a collaborative mindset are far more likely to stay together long term.

When the language changes from “you always…” to “how do we solve this?”, everything changes.

The next time a problem arises, pause and ask:

“How can we tackle this together?”

When challenges arise, do you feel like teammates or opponents?

Hack 14
Support Your Partner's Growth

One of the most powerful things you can do in a relationship is encourage your partner to grow.

Support their ambitions. Celebrate their goals. Be their loudest cheerleader.

When two people actively support each other's personal development, the relationship becomes a place of empowerment rather than limitation.

Psychological research shows that individuals who feel supported by their partner in pursuing personal goals experience greater life satisfaction and stronger relationship commitment.

This is where what I like to call **Power Couple Energy** begins.

Two people growing individually while supporting each other collectively.

Ask your partner:
"What's something you want to achieve this year that I can support you with?"

Does your partner feel encouraged to grow within your relationship?

Hack 15
Invest in Your Own Self-Improvement

Here's a truth many people overlook.

The healthiest relationships are built by two people who are both committed to becoming better versions of themselves.

If you grow emotionally, intellectually, and personally, the relationship grows with you.

When both partners invest in their personal development, they bring more awareness, resilience, and emotional intelligence into the partnership.

In psychology, this is known as **self-expansion theory** — the idea that relationships thrive when individuals continue growing rather than stagnating.

And yes, I will openly admit my bias here. I am a huge believer in self-development.

Choose one personal growth area to focus on this year:

- emotional intelligence
- communication skills
- stress management
- physical wellbeing

What is one area of personal growth that would improve your relationship if you worked on it?

Hack 16
Learn Conflict Resolution Skills

Conflict itself is not the problem.

Poor conflict management is.

All healthy relationships experience disagreement. Two people with different personalities, experiences, and opinions will inevitably see things differently.

What matters is how you handle those moments.

Research from the Gottman Institute shows that couples who learn healthy conflict management strategies have significantly stronger long-term relationships.

Healthy conflict includes:

- listening without interrupting
- avoiding personal attacks
- expressing feelings rather than accusations
- focusing on solutions rather than blame

Conflict handled well can actually strengthen a relationship.

The next time conflict arises, try starting with this phrase:

"I want to understand your perspective before I respond."

When conflict happens, does it bring you closer together or push you further apart?

Hack 17
Encourage Feedback

Most people are comfortable giving feedback at work.

But when it comes to relationships, feedback suddenly becomes uncomfortable.

Why?

Because relationships feel personal.

However, healthy relationships actually benefit from **constructive feedback**. It allows both partners to understand how their actions impact each other and provides an opportunity for growth.

One of the biggest problems I see in struggling relationships is that people stop giving honest feedback. Instead, they quietly tolerate small frustrations until they build into resentment.

Psychological research shows that couples who are able to discuss concerns openly and respectfully tend to resolve issues more effectively and maintain stronger emotional bonds.

Encouraging feedback creates a relationship environment where both partners feel safe to grow.

Ask your partner this question:
"Is there something I do that you wish I handled differently?"

Listen with curiosity rather than defensiveness.

Do you make it safe for your partner to give you honest feedback?

Amanda's Tough Love Truth:

Growth in relationships requires honesty. Avoiding feedback might feel easier in the moment, but it often leads to bigger problems later.

Hack 18
Practice Mutual Respect

Respect is the quiet foundation underneath every healthy relationship.

Love may bring two people together, but respect is what allows the relationship to remain healthy over time.

Respect shows up in the way partners speak to each other, handle disagreements, and acknowledge each other's opinions.

Even during conflict, respectful couples avoid behaviours that damage trust, such as name-calling, belittling, or dismissing each other's feelings.

Relationship researcher Dr John Gottman identified **contempt and disrespect** as two of the strongest predictors of relationship breakdown.

Healthy couples protect respect, even when emotions are running high.

The next time you disagree with your partner, focus on responding with this phrase:

"I see this differently, but I want to understand your perspective."

Do your disagreements feel respectful, or do they sometimes cross into criticism?

Hack 19
Foster Emotional Safety

Emotional safety is one of the most important ingredients in a strong relationship.

It means knowing that you can express your thoughts, feelings, and vulnerabilities without fear of being dismissed, criticised, or judged.

When emotional safety exists, people feel more comfortable being honest, open, and authentic.

Without emotional safety, partners often begin hiding their feelings to avoid conflict or rejection.

Over time, this creates emotional distance.

Research in relationship psychology consistently shows that couples who feel emotionally safe with each other experience higher levels of trust, intimacy, and long-term relationship satisfaction.

Ask your partner:
"Is there something you've been hesitant to talk to me about?"

Create space for an honest conversation.

Does your partner feel emotionally safe expressing their feelings with you?

“In many struggling relationships, partners are not avoiding honesty because they don’t care. They are avoiding honesty because they no longer feel emotionally safe.
Restoring that safety often changes everything.”

Hack 20
Cultivate Compassion

Compassion means responding to your partner with kindness and understanding, especially when they are struggling.

It involves recognising that everyone carries stress, fears, and challenges that may not always be visible.

One of the most powerful things you can offer your partner is the reassurance that they are not facing those challenges alone.

Compassion softens conflict, strengthens emotional connection, and helps partners feel supported even during difficult periods.

Research in emotional psychology shows that compassion strengthens relationship resilience by reducing defensiveness and increasing empathy.

In simple terms, compassion reminds both partners that they are on the same side.

The next time your partner seems stressed or overwhelmed, pause and ask:
"What can I do right now that would make your day a little easier?"

When your partner struggles, do you respond with frustration or compassion?

Amanda's Tough Love Truth:

Sometimes the most supportive thing you can do in a relationship is simply choose kindness.

Section 1 Exercise

The 10-Minute Connection Reset

Many couples tell me they struggle to find time to connect.

The truth is that connection doesn't require hours. It requires **intentional attention**.

This short exercise is designed to help you reconnect in just ten minutes.

How It Works

Set a timer for ten minutes.

During this time, one partner speaks while the other listens without interrupting.

Choose one of the following prompts:

- Something that has been on my mind lately is…
- One thing that made me feel good this week was…
- Something I've been feeling recently is…

The listening partner's only role is to listen and respond with curiosity.

Once the timer ends, switch roles.

The Goal

This exercise builds two important relationship skills:

- active listening
- emotional awareness

Even ten minutes of focused attention can strengthen emotional connection.

SECTION TWO: STRENGTHENING CONNECTION

"Love doesn't fade because people stop caring. It fades because people stop nurturing the connection."

Why This Section Matters

At the beginning of a relationship, connection often feels effortless.

Couples naturally spend time together, ask curious questions, and express affection regularly. There is excitement in discovering each other and building new memories together.

Over time, however, life becomes busier. Work, family responsibilities, and everyday pressures begin to take priority. Without realising it, couples may start spending more time managing responsibilities than nurturing the relationship itself.

This shift doesn't mean the love has disappeared. It simply means that the habits that once strengthened connection have become less frequent.

Connection thrives when couples intentionally create moments of appreciation, affection, curiosity, and shared experiences. Even small gestures can have a powerful impact on how partners feel about each other.

The hacks in this section are designed to help couples rekindle that sense of connection and keep the emotional bond alive.

Because when couples stay emotionally connected, the relationship becomes a source of energy, support, and joy rather than another responsibility to manage.

Amanda's Tough Love Truth:

Connection rarely disappears overnight. It fades when attention, appreciation, and curiosity slowly disappear too.

Why Connection Fades in Long-Term Relationships

Most couples don't lose connection overnight.

It usually happens gradually.

Life becomes busy. Work, family responsibilities, finances, and everyday pressures begin to take priority. Conversations become more about logistics than connection.

"What time are we leaving?"
"Did you pay that bill?"
"Can you pick up groceries on the way home?"

Over time, the relationship can quietly shift from being a place of emotional closeness to a place where life simply gets managed.

This doesn't mean the love has disappeared.

More often, it means the habits that once nurtured connection have slowly faded into the background.

In the early stages of a relationship, couples naturally prioritise connection. They spend time together, ask curious questions, show affection, and express appreciation.

But without intentional effort, those behaviours can gradually become less frequent.

Research in relationship psychology consistently shows that emotional connection thrives when couples maintain regular positive interactions.

These moments don't need to be grand or time-consuming.

A hug before leaving the house.
A genuine compliment.

A meaningful conversation at the end of the day.

Small moments of connection, repeated consistently, strengthen relationships over time.

The following hacks are designed to help you intentionally nurture that connection again.

Because when couples make connection a priority, relationships become lighter, more supportive, and far more enjoyable.

Amanda's Tough Love Truth:

Connection fades when couples stop investing in it. The good news is that it can be rebuilt the same way — through small, consistent acts of attention and care.

Hack 21
Express Appreciation

Feeling appreciated is one of the most powerful emotional experiences in a relationship.

Yet over time, many couples begin assuming their partner already knows they are valued. The compliments and gratitude that once flowed naturally in the early stages of a relationship often become less frequent.

Unfortunately, appreciation that goes unspoken can slowly disappear.

Research from positive psychology shows that expressing gratitude regularly strengthens emotional bonds and increases relationship satisfaction. When people feel appreciated, they are more likely to continue investing in the relationship.

Appreciation shifts the focus from what may be lacking to what is already meaningful and working well.

And sometimes, the simplest words can make the biggest difference.

Today, tell your partner one thing you genuinely appreciate about them that you may not have said recently.

When was the last time your partner heard you express appreciation for something they do?

Amanda's Tough Love Truth:

If appreciation disappears from a relationship, resentment often takes its place.

Hack 22
Celebrate Successes

Celebrating achievements together strengthens the sense that you are building a life as partners.

Too often, couples acknowledge major milestones but overlook everyday victories. Yet those smaller successes deserve recognition as well.

A challenging project completed.
A personal goal achieved.
A difficult week navigated successfully.

Research on supportive relationships shows that couples who celebrate each other's successes experience higher levels of trust and emotional closeness.

Celebration communicates something powerful:

"Your achievements matter to me."

When success becomes something shared rather than individual, the relationship becomes a source of encouragement rather than pressure.

Ask your partner:
"What's something you're proud of accomplishing recently?"
Celebrate it together, even if it seems small.

Do you regularly acknowledge and celebrate your partner's achievements?

Hack 23
Celebrate the Litte Things

While major milestones are exciting, the strength of a relationship is often built through everyday moments.

A kind message during the day.
A shared laugh.
Finishing a long week and relaxing together.

These moments might seem ordinary, but they are the threads that weave connection into daily life.

Relationship researcher Dr John Gottman found that couples who respond positively to each other's small attempts to connect build stronger long-term relationships.

These moments are known as **bids for connection**.

When one partner says something like, *"Look at this funny video,"* or *"You wouldn't believe what happened at work today,"* they are reaching out for connection.

Healthy couples respond to those moments.

The next time your partner shares something small, pause and engage fully rather than responding distractedly.

How often do you respond positively to your partner's everyday attempts to connect?

Hack 24
Prioritise Quality Time

Spending time together is important, but **how** you spend that time matters even more.

Many couples sit next to each other while scrolling on their phones, watching separate screens, or multitasking through conversations.

Technically they are together, but emotionally they are disconnected.

Quality time means giving your partner focused attention.

It might involve a walk together, a meal without distractions, or simply a meaningful conversation.

Studies on relationship satisfaction consistently show that couples who engage in intentional quality time report stronger emotional bonds.

Even small amounts of uninterrupted time can make a meaningful difference.

Schedule **one phone-free activity together this week,** even if it's just a short walk or coffee.

When you spend time together, are you truly present with each other?

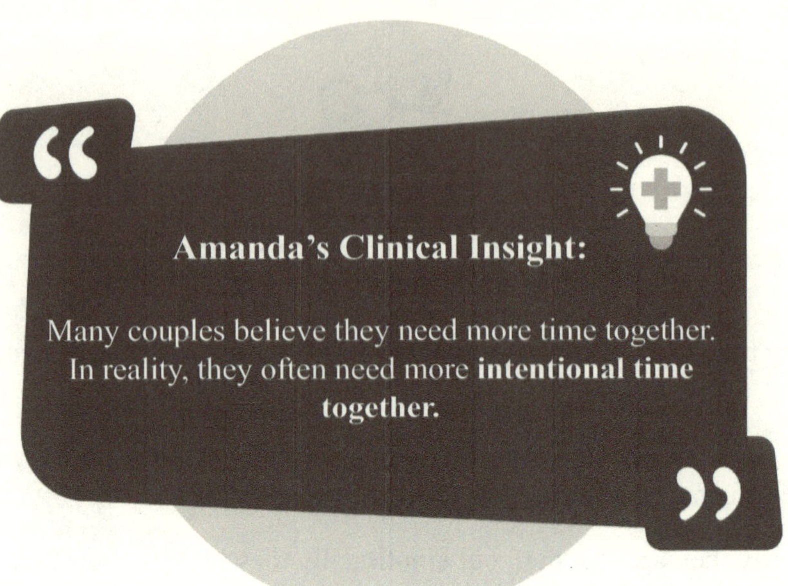
“
Amanda’s Clinical Insight:
Many couples believe they need more time together. In reality, they often need more **intentional time together.**
”

Hack 25
Show Physical Affection

Human connection isn't just emotional. It's physical as well.

Simple gestures like holding hands, hugging, or placing a reassuring hand on your partner's shoulder communicate warmth, care, and closeness.

Physical affection releases oxytocin, sometimes called the "bonding hormone," which helps reduce stress and increase feelings of connection.

In long-term relationships, physical affection can gradually decrease as routines take over daily life.

Reintroducing small moments of physical connection can have a powerful impact on emotional closeness.

Touch reminds your partner that they are loved, supported, and valued.

Offer your partner a 20-second hug today.

Longer hugs increase oxytocin and calm the nervous system.

Has physical affection increased or decreased in your relationship over time?

Hack 26
Foster Emotional Intimacy

Emotional intimacy is what allows couples to feel deeply connected.

It develops when partners share their thoughts, fears, hopes, and experiences openly with each other.

Without emotional intimacy, relationships can start to feel more like logistical partnerships than emotional ones.

Emotional intimacy grows through vulnerability.

When one partner shares something personal and the other responds with understanding and care, trust deepens.

Psychological research consistently shows that couples who maintain emotional intimacy experience stronger long-term relationship satisfaction.

True connection happens when both partners feel seen and understood.

Ask your partner this question tonight:
"What's something you've been thinking about a lot lately?"

Listen without interrupting.

Do you and your partner regularly talk about deeper thoughts and feelings?

Amanda's Tough Love Truth:

You cannot build deep connection while staying emotionally guarded.

Hack 27
Share Vulnerabilities

One of the strongest forms of connection in a relationship is vulnerability.

Sharing fears, insecurities, or worries can feel uncomfortable at first. Many people have spent years learning to protect those parts of themselves.

However, emotional intimacy grows when people allow their partner to see their authentic self.

When one partner opens up and the other responds with empathy and understanding, trust deepens. This type of openness creates emotional closeness that surface-level conversations simply cannot provide.

Psychological research shows that vulnerability strengthens relationships because it invites empathy and reinforces emotional safety.

In other words, vulnerability is not weakness. It is an invitation to deeper connection.

Share something small but personal with your partner today.

For example:
"Something I've been feeling unsure about lately is…"

Do you feel comfortable being emotionally open with your partner?

Amanda's Tough Love Truth:

If you never allow your partner to see your vulnerable side, you may also be preventing deeper connection.

Hack 28
Laugh Together Often

Laughter is one of the most underrated relationship skills.

Couples who laugh together regularly tend to feel more connected, more relaxed around each other, and more resilient during difficult moments.

Shared humour can diffuse tension, create joyful memories, and remind partners why they enjoy being around each other in the first place.

Research in relationship psychology shows that humour helps couples manage stress and strengthens emotional bonding.

It's not about being funny all the time. It's about allowing space for lightness and playfulness in the relationship.

Sometimes laughter is exactly what a relationship needs to reset.

Share something funny with your partner today. A story, a memory, or even a silly video.

Laugh together intentionally.

When was the last time you and your partner laughed together?

Hack 29
Offer Daily Compliments

Compliments are small but powerful relationship deposits.

They communicate admiration, appreciation, and affection.

In the early stages of relationships, compliments often come naturally. People notice and express admiration for each other frequently.

Over time, many couples assume those feelings are already understood and stop saying them out loud.

But hearing positive words from your partner continues to matter, even years into a relationship.

Relationship research consistently shows that positive verbal interactions strengthen emotional connection and increase relationship satisfaction.

Compliments remind your partner that they are still seen and valued.

Give your partner **one genuine compliment today.**

Make it specific.

When was the last time you told your partner something you admire about them?

Amanda's Tough Love Truth:

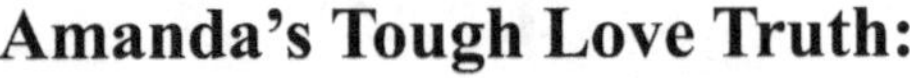

Never underestimate the power of feeling appreciated by the person you love.

Hack 30
Express Love and Affection

Love may be felt internally, but it still needs to be expressed.

Many people assume their partner simply knows they are loved. But hearing or seeing that love expressed can reinforce emotional security and connection.

Expressions of affection may include:

- saying "I love you"
- a warm hug
- a thoughtful message during the day
- a small act of kindness

These actions communicate reassurance and emotional closeness.

Research in attachment theory suggests that regular expressions of affection strengthen feelings of security within relationships.

Affection helps partners feel valued, supported, and emotionally connected.

Send your partner a message today that simply says:

"Just thinking about you."

How often do you intentionally express love to your partner?

Hack 31
Maintain Non-Verbal Connection

Communication isn't only about words.

Eye contact, tone of voice, facial expressions, and body language all communicate powerful messages within relationships.

A warm smile.
A reassuring touch.
Eye contact during conversation.

These small signals often communicate care and attention more strongly than words.

Non-verbal cues also help partners feel emotionally acknowledged and understood.

Studies on relationship communication show that positive non-verbal behaviours significantly influence how supported and connected partners feel.

Paying attention to these subtle forms of communication strengthens everyday connection.

During your next conversation, focus on maintaining eye contact and being fully present.

Do your non-verbal cues communicate warmth and attention to your partner?

Hack 32
Show Unconditional Support

One of the most powerful things you can offer your partner is the knowledge that you are in their corner.

Unconditional support means standing beside your partner during both the easy and difficult moments.

It means celebrating their successes and offering encouragement when things feel challenging.

Support does not require solving every problem. Often it simply means listening and reminding your partner that they are not alone.

Relationships become stronger when both partners feel supported in pursuing their goals and navigating life's challenges.

Support creates emotional security, and emotional security strengthens connection.

Ask your partner today:

"Is there anything going on right now where you'd like a little more support from me?"

Does your partner feel that you are consistently in their corner?

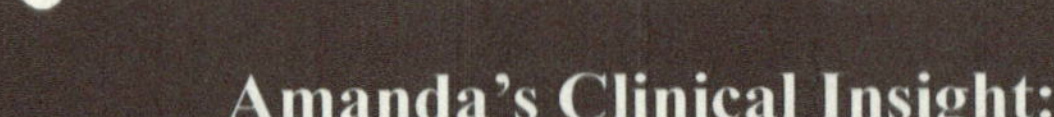

Amanda's Clinical Insight:

In many healthy relationships, partners describe their connection with a simple phrase: "We've got each other's back." That sense of partnership is incredibly powerful.

Hack 33
Stay Curious About Each Other

One of the most subtle shifts that happens in long-term relationships is that couples stop being curious about each other.

In the early stages of a relationship, curiosity is everywhere.

You want to know what your partner thinks about things, what excites them, what they dream about, and what their experiences have been.

But over time, many couples assume they already know everything about each other.

Here's the truth: people are constantly evolving.

Your partner today is not exactly the same person they were five years ago.

Healthy couples continue asking questions, exploring ideas, and learning about each other as they grow.

Curiosity keeps relationships feeling alive and interesting.

Ask your partner something you've never asked before.

For example:

"What's something you'd love to learn or try in the next few years?"

When was the last time you learned something new about your partner?

Amanda's Tough Love Truth:

If curiosity disappears from a relationship, connection often follows.

Hack 34
Express Interest in Your Partner's Passions

You don't have to share every interest with your partner.

But showing genuine interest in the things that excite them can significantly strengthen connection.

When your partner talks about something they enjoy, they are sharing a part of their identity.

Taking the time to listen, ask questions, or occasionally participate in those activities shows that you value what matters to them.

Many couples find that even trying a partner's hobby once can lead to new shared experiences and memories.

Supporting each other's passions encourages individuality while strengthening the relationship.

Ask your partner:

"What's something you enjoy that I haven't shown much interest in before?"

Do you show curiosity and encouragement toward the things your partner enjoys?

Hack 35
Share Joy in Each Other's Achievements

Healthy relationships are strengthened when partners celebrate not only their own successes, but also each other's.

Psychologists refer to this as **active constructive responding**.

In simple terms, it means responding enthusiastically when your partner shares good news.

Instead of simply saying "That's nice," you engage with their excitement.

You ask questions. You celebrate with them. You acknowledge the effort behind the achievement.

Research shows that couples who actively celebrate each other's positive experiences build stronger emotional bonds.

Joy shared becomes joy multiplied.

The next time your partner shares good news, respond with enthusiasm and ask:

"How did that feel for you?"

When your partner shares something positive, do you respond with genuine enthusiasm?

Amanda's Clinical Insight:

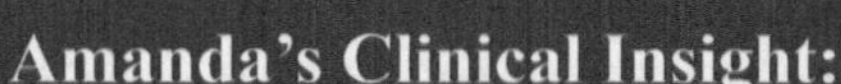

Some couples handle conflict well but overlook the importance of celebrating each other's positive moments. Those celebrations are powerful opportunities to strengthen connection.

Hack 36
Practice Mindfulness Together

Mindfulness simply means being present in the moment.

When couples practice mindfulness together, they create space to slow down and reconnect with each other.

This might involve simple activities such as:

- going for a walk together
- sharing a quiet coffee in the morning
- practicing meditation or breathing exercises
- spending a few minutes reflecting on the day

These moments allow partners to step away from distractions and reconnect with each other.

Research shows that mindfulness practices can reduce stress, increase emotional awareness, and improve communication within relationships.

Even a few minutes of shared mindfulness can strengthen emotional connection.

Spend five minutes together today without phones, distractions, or conversation. Simply sit together and be present.

How often do you and your partner intentionally slow down together?

Hack 37
Create Physical Connection Rituals

Physical affection becomes even more meaningful when it becomes a consistent ritual.

Small habits like hugging hello and goodbye, holding hands during a walk, or sharing a quick kiss before leaving the house can strengthen connection throughout the day.

These rituals create moments of reassurance and closeness that reinforce emotional bonds.

Over time, they become comforting signals of love and partnership.

Many couples underestimate the impact of these small rituals until they disappear.

But when they are present, they quietly reinforce the relationship every day.

Choose one simple physical connection ritual to practice daily.

For example:
- hug for 20 seconds before leaving the house
- hold hands during a walk
- kiss goodnight every evening

What small physical rituals already exist in your relationship?

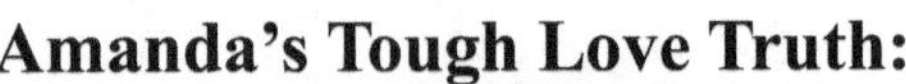

Amanda's Tough Love Truth:

Connection doesn't require grand gestures. It thrives on small habits repeated consistently.

Hack 38
Show Affection During Stressful Moments

Stress has a way of pulling couples apart.

When people feel overwhelmed by work, responsibilities, or external pressures, they sometimes withdraw emotionally from their partner.

Ironically, these stressful moments are often when connection matters most.

Offering affection during stressful times communicates support and reassurance.

A hug, a kind word, or simply sitting beside your partner while they talk through something difficult can help them feel less alone.

Studies in relationship psychology show that supportive responses during stressful periods strengthen long-term relationship resilience.

In other words, the way couples show up for each other during difficult times often defines the strength of the relationship.

When your partner seems stressed, pause and ask:

"Do you need advice, or would you prefer me to just listen?"

How do you usually respond when your partner is feeling overwhelmed?

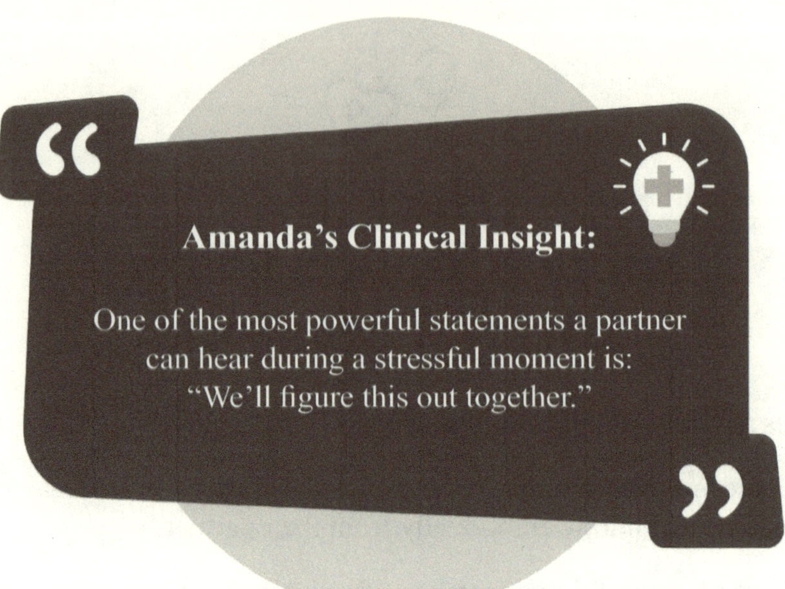
Amanda's Clinical Insight:
One of the most powerful statements a partner can hear during a stressful moment is: "We'll figure this out together."

Hack 39
Practice Gratitude Together

Gratitude has a powerful impact on relationships.

When couples regularly acknowledge what they appreciate about each other and their shared life, the emotional tone of the relationship becomes more positive.

Instead of focusing on frustrations or what may be missing, gratitude shifts attention toward what is already meaningful and working well.

Psychological research shows that gratitude increases relationship satisfaction, strengthens emotional bonds, and reduces negativity within partnerships.

When gratitude becomes a shared habit, both partners begin noticing more of the positive contributions the other person brings to the relationship.

Gratitude also reinforces the idea that the relationship itself is something worth appreciating.

Before going to bed tonight, each partner shares **one thing they appreciated about the other person that day.**

How often do you and your partner intentionally acknowledge what you appreciate about each other?

"

Amanda's Clinical Insight: 

In many struggling relationships, appreciation has quietly disappeared. When couples begin expressing gratitude again, the emotional atmosphere of the relationship often shifts surprisingly quickly.

"

Hack 40
Create Emotional Check-In Rituals

Many couples regularly check their schedules, finances, and responsibilities.

But they rarely check the emotional health of their relationship.

Creating a regular emotional check-in ritual allows couples to stay connected and aware of how each person is feeling.

These conversations provide space to discuss concerns, celebrate progress, and ensure that both partners feel supported.

Check-ins do not need to be long or complicated.

Even a short weekly conversation can help partners stay aligned and prevent small frustrations from building into larger problems.

One simple approach is the **Traffic Light Check-In**, which I often use with couples.

- **Green:** Things that are going well
- **Yellow:** Things that may need adjusting
- **Red:** Things that need to stop

This framework creates a clear and respectful way for couples to discuss what is happening in the relationship.

Schedule a **weekly relationship check-in** and ask each other:

- What felt good in our relationship this week?
- Is there anything we should adjust?
- What can we do to support each other this week?

When was the last time you intentionally talked about the health of your relationship?

Amanda's Tough Love Truth:

Relationships rarely fall apart because couples talked too much about how they were feeling.
More often, they struggle because important conversations never happened.

Section 2 Exercise

The Appreciation Conversation

Over time, many couples begin focusing on what their partner is **not doing**, rather than what they **are doing**.

This exercise shifts the focus back to appreciation.

How It Works

Each partner takes turns answering the following questions.

1. One thing I appreciate about you is…
2. Something you do that makes my life easier is…
3. One quality I admire in you is…

The key rule: **no deflecting compliments**.

Simply receive them and say "thank you."

The Goal

This exercise strengthens emotional connection and reminds both partners that they are valued.

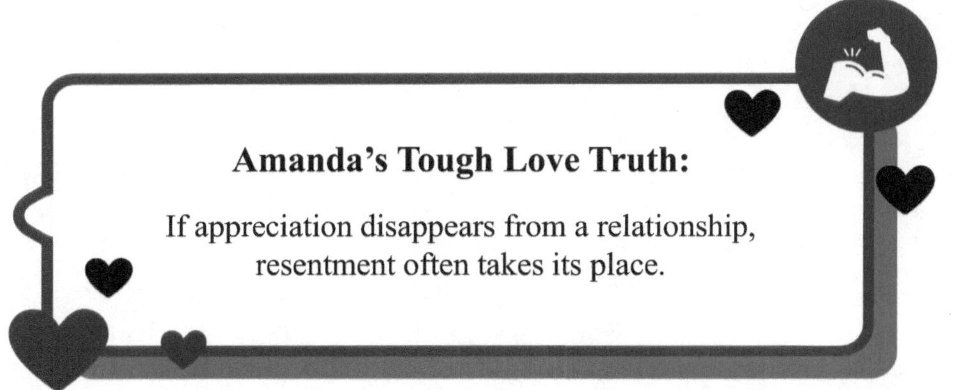

SECTION THREE:
NAVIGATING CONFLICT AND REPAIR

"Conflict isn't the enemy of a relationship. Silence, resentment, and poor communication are."

Why This Section Matters

Every relationship experiences conflict.

Two individuals with different perspectives, personalities, and life experiences will inevitably disagree from time to time. The presence of conflict does not mean a relationship is failing. In fact, disagreement can often lead to deeper understanding when handled well.

The real challenge lies in how couples respond to conflict.

Many people enter relationships without having learned healthy conflict skills. Instead, they may rely on patterns they observed growing up, such as avoidance, defensiveness, or criticism.

When conflict is handled poorly, it can lead to emotional distance, resentment, and ongoing misunderstandings.

But when couples develop the ability to navigate disagreements with respect and empathy, conflict can become an opportunity for growth rather than damage.

The hacks in this section provide practical strategies to help couples manage conflict constructively, repair emotional ruptures, and maintain respect even during difficult conversations.

Learning how to handle conflict well is one of the most powerful investments couples can make in the longevity of their relationship.

Amanda's Tough Love Truth:

The problem isn't that couples argue. The problem is when they never learn how to argue well.

Why Conflict Happens in Relationships

Every relationship experiences conflict…or better yet, let's call this a 'difference of opinions'.

Two people with different personalities, backgrounds, experiences, and perspectives are naturally going to see things differently from time to time.

The problem isn't disagreement.

The problem occurs when couples lack the skills to handle those disagreements in a healthy way.

Many people grew up without witnessing effective conflict resolution. Instead, they may have seen avoidance, criticism, shouting, or emotional withdrawal.

Without realizing it, these patterns can follow us into our own relationships.

The encouraging news is that **conflict resolution is a skill that can be learned**.

Healthy couples don't avoid conflict. They simply learn how to handle it in ways that strengthen rather than damage the relationship.

The hacks in this section will help you do exactly that.

Amanda's Tough Love Truth:

Avoiding conflict doesn't protect a relationship.
Learning how to handle it does.

Hack 41
Resolve Conflict Constructively

When conflict arises, couples often fall into one of two traps.

They either escalate quickly into arguments, or they avoid the issue entirely.

Neither approach is particularly helpful.

Constructive conflict focuses on understanding the issue and working toward a solution together.

This means staying calm, listening actively, and focusing on the problem rather than attacking each other personally.

Relationship research shows that couples who approach conflict collaboratively tend to experience stronger emotional bonds and greater long-term stability.

Constructive conflict transforms disagreement into an opportunity for growth.

The next time a disagreement arises, pause and say:
"Let's slow down and figure this out together."

During disagreements, do you focus on solving the problem or proving your point?

Hack 42
Learn Conflict Resolution Skills

Conflict resolution isn't something most people are formally taught.

In fact, many couples enter relationships assuming that love alone will somehow make conflict easier to manage.

Unfortunately, love doesn't automatically teach communication skills.

Effective conflict resolution includes several important behaviours:

- listening without interrupting
- expressing feelings rather than accusations
- seeking understanding before reacting
- focusing on solutions rather than blame

Relationship expert Dr John Gottman's research suggests that the ability to manage conflict constructively is one of the strongest predictors of long-term relationship success.

These skills take practice, but they are absolutely learnable.

During your next disagreement, replace "you always" with: "When this happens, I feel…"

Were healthy conflict skills modelled in the relationships you observed growing up?

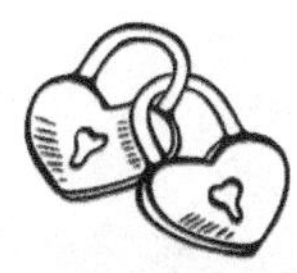

Hack 43
De-escalate Conflict Early

Conflict often escalates because emotions rise faster than communication skills.

A small disagreement can quickly grow into a heated argument when partners feel unheard or attacked.

Learning to recognise the early signs of escalation is incredibly valuable.

These signs might include:

- raised voices
- defensive body language
- interrupting each other
- repeating the same points

When escalation begins, the most helpful step is often to pause.

Taking a short break allows both partners to calm their nervous systems before continuing the conversation.

Research in emotional regulation shows that people communicate more effectively once they have had time to cool down.

If a discussion begins escalating, say:

"I care about this conversation. Let's take a short break and come back to it calmly."

What signs tell you that a conversation is becoming emotionally heated?

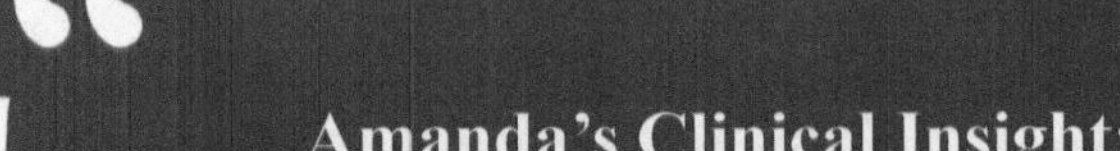

Amanda's Clinical Insight:

Many couples believe taking a break during conflict means avoiding the issue. In reality, it often allows the conversation to continue more productively later.

Hack 44
Apologise Sincerely

Apologising is one of the most powerful ways to repair a relationship after conflict.

Unfortunately, many apologies fall into the category of **non-apologies**, such as:

"I'm sorry you feel that way."

A sincere apology takes responsibility for one's actions and acknowledges the impact those actions had on the other person.

A meaningful apology usually includes:

- acknowledging the mistake
- expressing genuine regret
- committing to doing better next time

When apologies are sincere, they rebuild trust and restore emotional connection.

The next time you apologise, try this structure:

"I'm sorry for ___. I understand that it made you feel ___. I will work on doing better."

Do your apologies focus on repairing the relationship, or on defending your actions?

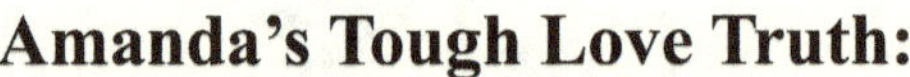

Amanda's Tough Love Truth:

A sincere apology repairs relationships. A defensive apology often makes things worse.

Hack 45
Practice Forgiveness

Every long-term relationship requires forgiveness.

People make mistakes. They say things they regret. They misunderstand each other.

Holding onto resentment can quietly damage emotional connection over time.

Forgiveness does not mean ignoring hurtful behaviour or pretending something didn't matter.

It means choosing to release the emotional burden of resentment so the relationship can move forward.

Research in emotional wellbeing shows that forgiveness reduces stress, improves mental health, and strengthens relationships.

Forgiveness allows couples to grow rather than remain stuck in past mistakes.

Reflect on a past disagreement and ask yourself:

"Am I holding onto something that I could choose to let go of?"

Is there a past issue in your relationship that still needs healing?

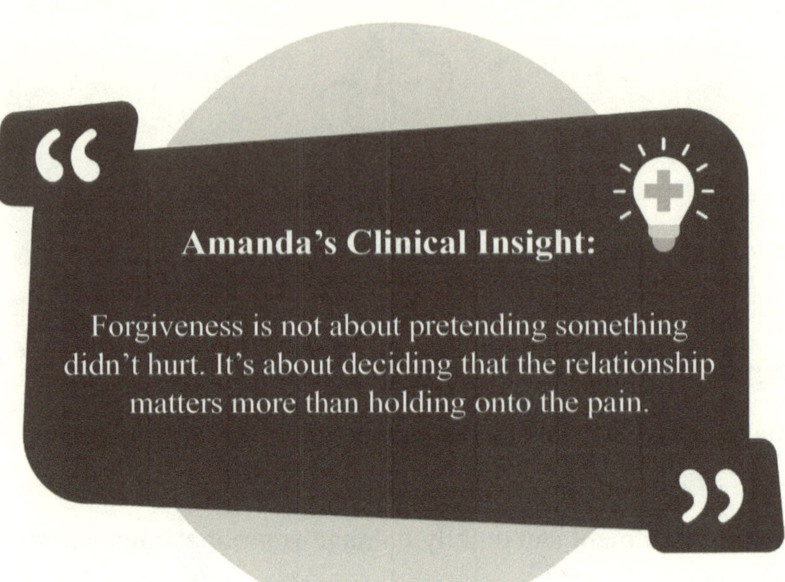
Amanda's Clinical Insight:
Forgiveness is not about pretending something didn't hurt. It's about deciding that the relationship matters more than holding onto the pain.

A Story About Conflict

A couple once came into my office convinced they had a "communication problem."

They had been together for nearly fifteen years and described themselves as arguing about the same issues over and over again.

One partner felt unheard.
The other felt constantly criticised.

During one session they began describing a disagreement about something small…who was responsible for organising a family event.

Within minutes the conversation escalated.

Voices raised.
Frustration grew.
Both partners tried to explain why they were right.

Eventually I asked them to pause.

I then asked a simple question.

"Are you trying to win the argument, or are you trying to improve the relationship?"

The room went quiet.

After a moment, one of them laughed and said, "Right now… probably win the argument."

That moment changed everything.

Because they realised something important: they weren't actually fighting about the event anymore. They were fighting about **feeling unheard and unappreciated**.

Once they learned a few simple communication and conflict skills, the dynamic between them shifted.

They started listening more carefully.
They paused when conversations escalated.
They focused on solving problems together rather than blaming each other.

The arguments didn't disappear completely. No relationship is conflict-free.

But they became **shorter, calmer, and far less damaging**.

This is what healthy conflict looks like.

Not the absence of disagreement.

But the presence of skills that help couples move through those disagreements with respect and understanding.

Amanda's Tough Love Truth:

Most couples don't argue too much.

They simply haven't learned **how to argue well**.

Hack 46
Offer Constructive Feedback

Feedback in relationships can be incredibly valuable, when it's delivered in the right way.

The goal of constructive feedback is to encourage growth, not criticism.

Healthy feedback focuses on behaviour rather than attacking the person.

For example, there is a big difference between saying:

"You're always so inconsiderate."

and

"When this happens, it makes me feel overlooked."

Constructive feedback invites conversation and improvement rather than defensiveness.

Relationship research consistently shows that couples who express concerns respectfully are far more likely to resolve issues successfully.

When giving feedback, use this simple formula:

"When ___ happens, I feel ___. I would appreciate if we could try ___."

When you raise concerns with your partner, do they feel like an attack or an invitation to improve together?

Hack 47
Address Jealousy Quickly

Jealousy can appear in many relationships.

Sometimes it arises from insecurity, past experiences, or fear of losing the relationship.

Left unaddressed, jealousy can quietly erode trust and create unnecessary tension between partners.

Healthy couples treat jealousy as a signal for conversation rather than accusation.

Instead of making assumptions, they discuss what they are feeling and why.

Open communication helps partners reassure each other and clarify misunderstandings before the issue grows larger.

Addressing jealousy early prevents it from turning into resentment or suspicion.

If jealousy arises, start the conversation with honesty: "I've been feeling a little insecure about something, and I'd like to talk about it."

When feelings of jealousy arise, do you communicate them openly or keep them to yourself?

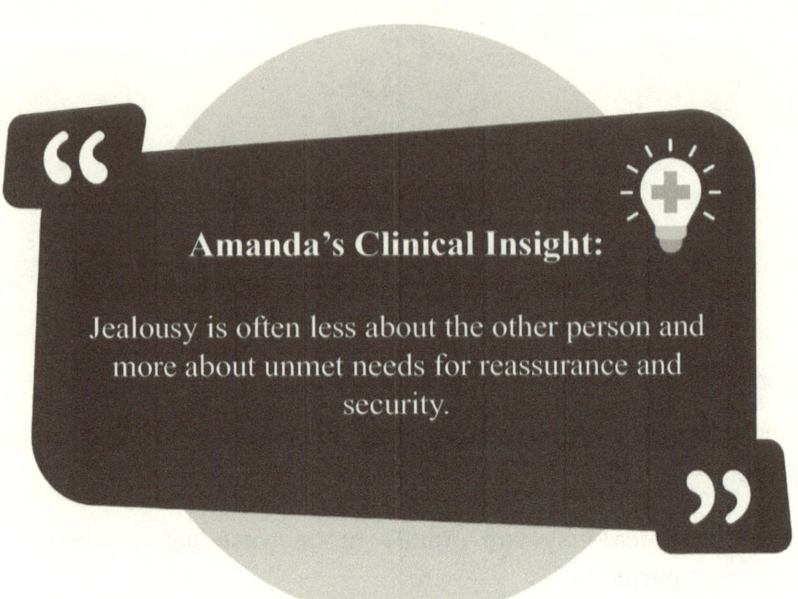
Amanda's Clinical Insight:
Jealousy is often less about the other person and more about unmet needs for reassurance and security.

Hack 48
Discuss Needs Regularly

Many relationship frustrations stem from **unspoken needs**.

Partners may hope the other person will notice what they need without having to say it directly.

Unfortunately, this expectation often leads to disappointment.

Healthy couples regularly talk about their needs, whether those needs relate to emotional support, personal space, affection, or practical responsibilities.

Needs can change over time as life circumstances evolve.

By discussing them openly, couples avoid misunderstandings and ensure both partners feel valued and supported.

Ask your partner:

"What's one thing that would help you feel more supported right now?"

Do you clearly express your needs in the relationship?

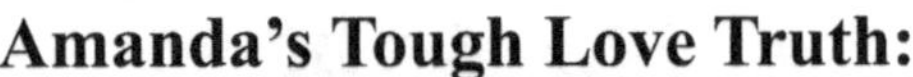

Amanda's Tough Love Truth:

Your partner cannot meet needs they never hear about.

Hack 49
Create a Safe Word for Arguments

Some couples find it helpful to create a simple signal that indicates a conversation has become too heated.

This might be a word or phrase that both partners agree will pause the discussion when emotions begin escalating.

The purpose is not to avoid the issue, but to prevent the conversation from becoming destructive.

Once the safe word is used, both partners agree to pause the discussion, take time to calm down, and return to the conversation later.

This strategy can prevent arguments from spiralling into hurtful exchanges.

Choose a neutral word together that signals the need for a pause during heated discussions.

What signs tell you that an argument is becoming unproductive?

Hack 50
Handle Stress as a Team

Stress is inevitable.

Work pressures, financial concerns, family responsibilities, and unexpected life challenges can all place strain on a relationship.

The key difference between struggling couples and thriving couples is how they handle stress together.

Healthy partners support each other during difficult times rather than withdrawing or blaming.

They check in, offer encouragement, and remind each other that they are facing challenges together.

Stress becomes far more manageable when partners feel supported rather than alone.

Ask your partner:
"What has been the most stressful part of your week?"

Then listen without trying to immediately fix the problem.

Do stressful periods bring you and your partner closer together or create distance?

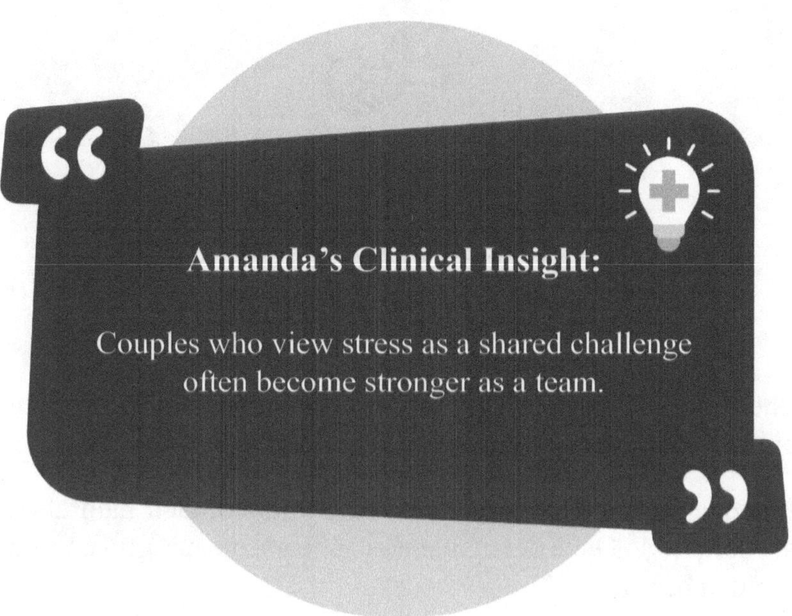
Amanda's Clinical Insight:
Couples who view stress as a shared challenge often become stronger as a team.

Hack 51
Implement a No-Judgement Rule

One of the quickest ways to shut down communication in a relationship is judgement.

When someone feels judged, criticised, or dismissed, their natural response is to become defensive. Once defensiveness appears, meaningful communication becomes much harder.

Healthy couples work hard to create an environment where both partners feel safe expressing their thoughts and feelings without fear of being ridiculed or invalidated.

This doesn't mean partners must always agree with each other. It simply means approaching conversations with curiosity rather than judgement.

When couples practice a "no judgement" approach, they create space for honesty and vulnerability.

And honesty is the foundation of strong communication.

The next time your partner shares something personal, resist the urge to immediately evaluate or correct.

Instead say:
"Thank you for sharing that with me."

Do your responses encourage your partner to open up, or to shut down?

Amanda's Tough Love Truth:

Judgement rarely improves communication. Curiosity almost always does.

Hack 52
Communicate Expectations Clearly

Many relationship frustrations arise from mismatched expectations.

One partner may expect certain behaviours, responsibilities, or forms of support without ever communicating them directly.

When those expectations aren't met, disappointment appears.

Clear expectations remove guesswork from the relationship.

Healthy couples talk openly about what they hope for in areas such as:

- responsibilities at home
- emotional support
- time together
- communication habits
- boundaries with others

Discussing expectations doesn't make a relationship rigid. It makes it clearer.

Clarity reduces misunderstanding.

Ask your partner:

"Is there something you expected from me recently that we may not have discussed clearly?"

Have you ever felt disappointed because an expectation was never communicated?

Hack 53
Validate Each Other's Feelings

Validation is one of the most powerful communication tools in relationships.

It means acknowledging your partner's emotional experience, even if you don't fully agree with their perspective.

Validation does not mean saying your partner is right.

It means saying that their feelings are understandable.

For example:

"I can see why that upset you."

Statements like this can dramatically reduce defensiveness during conflict.

When people feel heard and understood, they are more willing to listen in return.

Research on emotional regulation shows that validation can help calm emotional responses and promote more constructive conversations.

The next time your partner expresses frustration, respond with:

"That makes sense. I can understand why you'd feel that way."

How often do you focus on understanding your partner's feelings before responding?

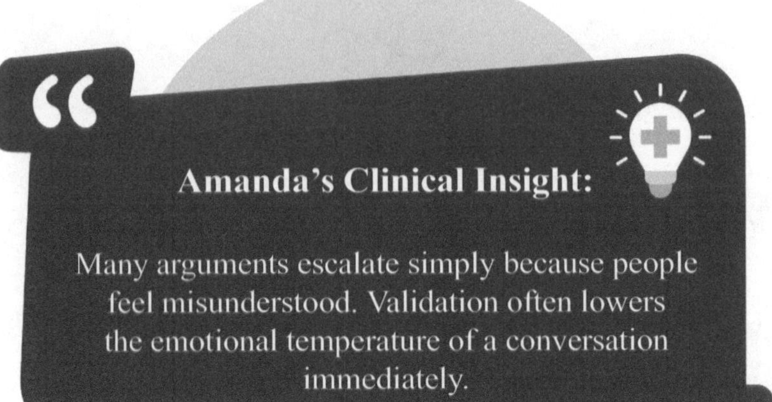
Amanda's Clinical Insight:
Many arguments escalate simply because people feel misunderstood. Validation often lowers the emotional temperature of a conversation immediately.

Hack 54
Recognise Emotional Triggers

Emotional triggers are powerful reactions connected to past experiences.

Sometimes a partner's behaviour unintentionally activates an emotional response linked to previous relationships, childhood experiences, or personal insecurities.

When triggers are not recognised, reactions can seem disproportionate to the situation.

Understanding triggers allows couples to approach these moments with empathy rather than confusion or blame.

Healthy couples become curious about what lies beneath strong emotional reactions.

Recognising triggers allows both partners to respond more thoughtfully rather than reacting impulsively.

Reflect on the following question:

"When I feel strongly triggered in conflict, what deeper fear or experience might be influencing my reaction?"

Are there certain topics or behaviours that consistently trigger strong reactions in your relationship?

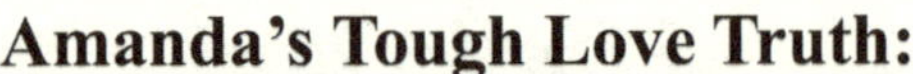

Amanda's Tough Love Truth:

Sometimes the argument you're having today is actually connected to an old wound from the past.

Hack 55
Avoid Criticism and Contempt

Relationship researcher Dr John Gottman identified several behaviours that are particularly damaging to relationships.

Two of the most harmful are **criticism and contempt**.

Criticism attacks a person's character rather than addressing a specific behaviour.

Contempt includes behaviours such as sarcasm, eye rolling, mocking, or belittling.

These behaviours erode respect and create emotional distance.

Healthy couples focus on discussing specific behaviours rather than attacking each other personally.

For example:

Instead of:
"You're so irresponsible."

Try:
"I felt stressed when that didn't get done."

The difference may seem small, but it dramatically changes the tone of the conversation.

Respectful communication protects the emotional safety of the relationship.

During your next disagreement, focus on describing how a behaviour affected you rather than criticising your partner's character.

When conflict arises, do your words focus on the behaviour or the person?

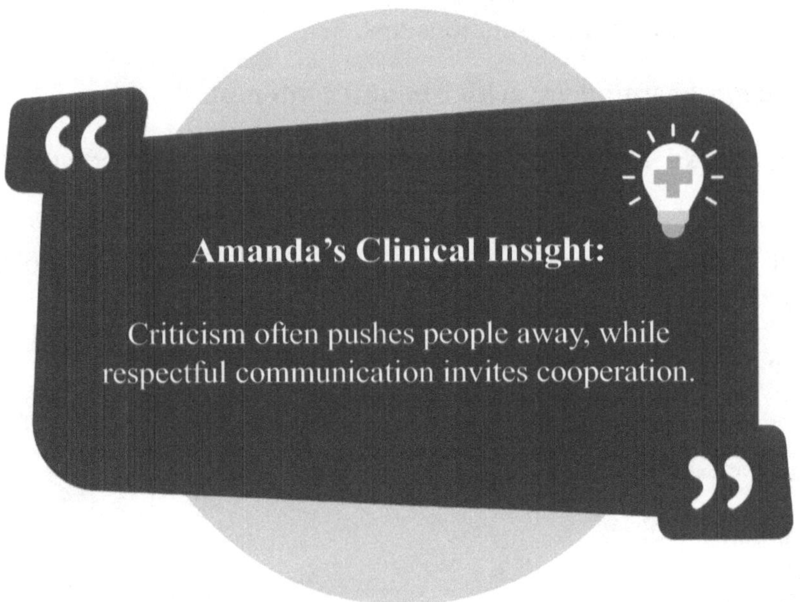

Hack 56
Revisit Conflicts Calmly

Not every conflict gets resolved in the moment.

Sometimes emotions run too high, misunderstandings pile up, or both partners simply need time to process what has happened.

Revisiting a disagreement once emotions have settled can often lead to a much more productive conversation.

Healthy couples understand that stepping away temporarily does not mean abandoning the issue. It means allowing space for reflection so the conversation can continue more calmly later.

When couples revisit conflicts thoughtfully, they often gain clarity about what really mattered beneath the disagreement.

If a conversation ends unresolved, revisit it later by saying: "I'd like us to talk about what happened earlier so we can understand each other better."

Do you tend to avoid revisiting disagreements, or are you willing to return to them calmly?

Hack 57
Repair Emotional Ruptures Quickly

Even the healthiest couples occasionally hurt each other.

A harsh tone, a dismissive comment, or an argument that goes too far can create what psychologists call an **emotional rupture**.

What matters most is how quickly the relationship is repaired.

Research shows that couples who repair emotional ruptures effectively tend to maintain stronger long-term relationships.

Repair attempts might include:

- apologising sincerely
- acknowledging hurt feelings
- offering reassurance
- expressing a desire to reconnect

Repair does not erase what happened, but it restores the emotional safety that allows the relationship to move forward.

If a conversation ended poorly, send a message such as: "I don't like how that conversation ended. I care about you and would like us to talk again when we're both calm."

How quickly do you and your partner usually attempt to repair connection after conflict?

Amanda's Tough Love Truth:

Healthy couples don't avoid mistakes.
They repair them quickly.

Hack 58
Develop Collaborative Problem Solving

Conflict becomes much easier to navigate when couples approach problems as a team.

Collaborative problem solving focuses on finding solutions that work for both partners rather than forcing one person to "win" the argument.

This approach requires openness, compromise, and a willingness to consider each other's perspectives.

When couples work together to solve problems, they strengthen the sense that the relationship is a partnership.

The goal becomes progress rather than victory.

During a disagreement, ask your partner:
"What would a solution that works for both of us look like?"

Do your conflicts tend to focus on winning the argument or solving the problem together?

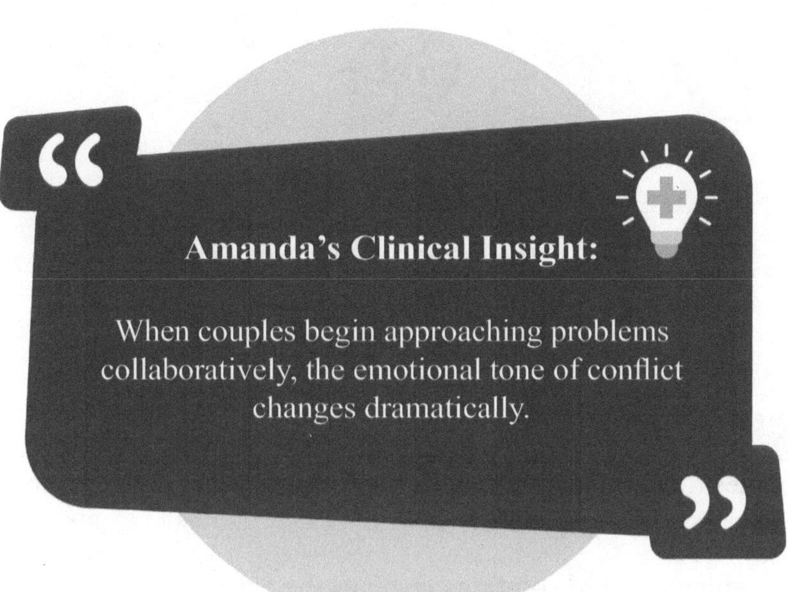
Amanda's Clinical Insight:
When couples begin approaching problems collaboratively, the emotional tone of conflict changes dramatically.

Hack 59
Focus on Solutions Rather Than Blame

Blame rarely leads to progress.

When couples focus on blaming each other for problems, conversations quickly become defensive and unproductive.

Shifting the focus toward solutions changes the entire dynamic.

Instead of dwelling on what went wrong, partners begin asking what can be improved moving forward.

This mindset encourages responsibility, growth, and cooperation.

It also prevents couples from becoming stuck in cycles of repeated arguments about past mistakes.

When discussing a challenge, ask:

"What can we do differently next time?"

Do your conversations focus more on the past problem or the future solution?

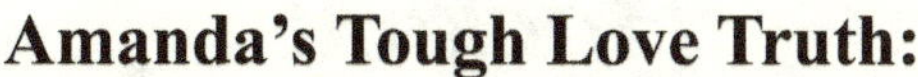

Amanda's Tough Love Truth:

Blame keeps couples stuck.
Solutions move relationships forward.

Hack 60
Practice Emotional Regulation

One of the most important skills in conflict is learning how to regulate emotions.

When people feel overwhelmed, their brain shifts into a defensive state that makes rational communication much harder.

Heart rate increases.
Voices rise.
Listening disappears.

Learning to recognise and manage these emotional responses can transform how couples handle conflict.

Simple strategies such as deep breathing, pausing conversations, or taking a short walk can help calm the nervous system and restore clear thinking.

When partners regulate their emotions effectively, they communicate with far greater clarity and respect.

If you feel overwhelmed during an argument, pause and take five slow breaths before continuing the conversation.

How do you typically respond when emotions run high during conflict?

Emotional regulation is not about suppressing feelings. It is about managing them in ways that allow communication to remain respectful and constructive.

Section 3 Exercise

The Conflict Reset Conversation

Conflict becomes destructive when emotions escalate faster than communication skills.

This exercise helps couples reset a difficult conversation.

How It Works

Choose a calm moment, not during an active argument.

Each partner answers the following questions.

1. One thing I wish you understood about my perspective is…
2. One thing I could have handled better during our disagreement was…
3. One thing I appreciate about how you handled the situation is…

The focus is **understanding, not winning**.

The Goal

This conversation builds empathy and reduces lingering resentment.

SECTION FOUR: GROWING TOGETHER

"Healthy relationships don't stand still. The strongest couples grow individually while supporting each other along the way."

Why This Section Matters

Relationships are not static.

Over time, people grow, change, and develop new perspectives. Careers evolve, interests shift, and personal priorities may change as life unfolds.

When couples fail to acknowledge or support these changes, the relationship can begin to feel restrictive or disconnected.

Healthy relationships create space for both partners to continue growing as individuals while also strengthening the partnership.

Growth might involve learning new skills, pursuing personal goals, exploring new interests, or simply becoming more emotionally aware.

Couples who encourage each other's growth often feel inspired by the relationship rather than limited by it.

The hacks in this section focus on how couples can evolve together, support each other's ambitions, and remain curious about who their partner is becoming over time.

When partners grow together, the relationship continues to feel dynamic, engaging, and meaningful.

Amanda's Tough Love Truth:

If only one person keeps growing, eventually the relationship stops moving forward.

Why Growth Matters in Relationships

One of the most exciting parts of a relationship is the opportunity to grow together.

But growth can also feel uncomfortable at times.

People evolve throughout life. Careers change, interests shift, goals develop, and personal priorities evolve. If couples stop supporting each other's growth, the relationship can begin to feel limiting rather than inspiring.

Healthy couples understand that growth is not a threat to the relationship.

It's an opportunity to strengthen it.

When partners support each other's ambitions, encourage learning, and remain curious about each other's evolving interests, the relationship becomes a place where both people can flourish.

Relationships that grow together remain vibrant, interesting, and resilient over time.

Amanda's Tough Love Truth:

A relationship should never feel like a cage.
It should feel like a place where both people are encouraged to grow.

Hack 61
Support Your Partner's Growth

One of the most meaningful things you can offer your partner is encouragement as they pursue personal growth.

Whether that growth involves career development, learning new skills, improving health, or exploring new interests, feeling supported by a partner can make a powerful difference.

Research in relationship psychology shows that individuals who feel encouraged by their partner in pursuing personal goals report higher relationship satisfaction and stronger emotional bonds.

Supporting growth means celebrating your partner's ambitions rather than feeling threatened by them.

It communicates a simple but powerful message:

"I believe in you."

Ask your partner:

"Is there something you'd like to improve or learn this year that I can support you with?"

Do you actively encourage your partner's personal growth?

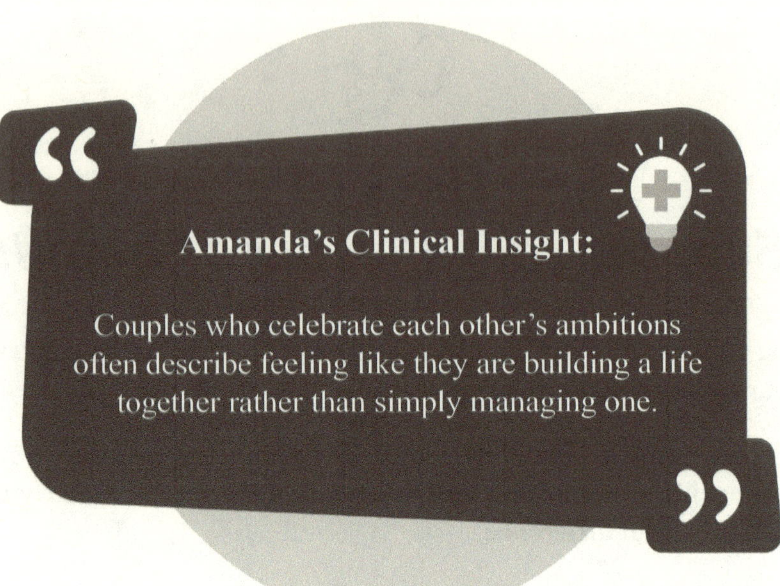
Amanda's Clinical Insight:
Couples who celebrate each other's ambitions often describe feeling like they are building a life together rather than simply managing one.

Hack 62
Encourage Each Other's Passions

Passions give people energy.

They bring excitement, creativity, and personal fulfilment into life.

When partners encourage each other's passions, they reinforce individuality while strengthening the relationship.

This might include supporting hobbies, creative pursuits, career ambitions, or personal projects.

You don't have to share every interest to support it.

Sometimes encouragement alone is enough to help your partner feel valued and understood.

Healthy relationships create space for both partners to explore what brings them joy.

Ask your partner:

"What's something you love doing that we haven't talked about in a while?"

Do you actively support the things that excite your partner?

Hack 63
Develop Mutual Goals

While individual growth is important, shared goals help couples feel aligned in the direction their relationship is heading.

Mutual goals might include:

- financial goals
- travel plans
- family plans
- lifestyle aspirations
- personal development goals

Working toward shared goals creates a sense of partnership and purpose.

It reminds both partners that they are building something meaningful together.

Research shows that couples who discuss long-term goals regularly tend to experience stronger relationship commitment.

Shared vision strengthens shared effort.

Ask each other:

"What is one goal we would love to achieve together in the next few years?"

Do you and your partner regularly discuss your future goals together?

Amanda's Tough Love Truth:

Couples who stop planning their future together often start drifting apart.

Hack 64
Learn Together

Learning something new together can be incredibly energising for a relationship.

It creates shared experiences, stimulates curiosity, and encourages teamwork.

Learning might involve:

- taking a class together
- exploring a new hobby
- reading and discussing books
- attending workshops
- developing new skills

These experiences create fresh memories and help couples see each other in new ways.

Learning together also encourages both partners to remain mentally engaged and curious.

Growth becomes something the relationship participates in together.

Choose something new to learn together this year.

It could be a language, cooking skill, dance class, or creative activity.

When was the last time you and your partner learned something new together?

Amanda's Clinical Insight:
Shared learning experiences often bring back the curiosity and excitement that couples felt in the early stages of their relationship.

Hack 65
Share Personal Histories

Understanding each other's past can deepen emotional connection in powerful ways.

Our experiences shape how we see the world, how we handle stress, and how we respond in relationships.

Sharing stories about childhood, formative experiences, and personal challenges helps partners understand each other more deeply.

These conversations often reveal insights that explain behaviours or reactions within the relationship.

Healthy couples remain interested in learning about each other's life stories, even years into the relationship.

Ask your partner:

"What is one childhood memory that shaped who you are today?"

How well do you understand the experiences that shaped your partner's perspective on life?

Hack 66
Encourage Intellectual Discussions

Healthy relationships thrive when partners engage not only emotionally, but intellectually as well.

Conversations about ideas, perspectives, and beliefs can stimulate curiosity and deepen understanding between partners.

Intellectual discussions might involve topics such as:

- current events
- personal values
- books or articles you've read
- life philosophies
- social or cultural ideas

These conversations allow partners to explore how each other thinks and evolves.

Over time, intellectual curiosity keeps relationships feeling fresh and engaging.

It also helps couples better understand the perspectives that shape each other's decisions and opinions.

Ask your partner:

"What's something you've been thinking about recently that we haven't talked about?"

Do your conversations regularly explore ideas and perspectives beyond daily logistics?

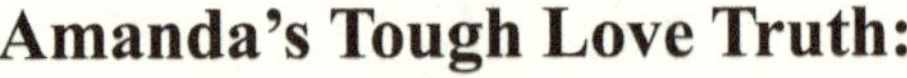

Amanda's Tough Love Truth:

If the only conversations you have are about schedules and responsibilities, connection will slowly fade.

Hack 67
Create Curiosity About Each Other's Work

Work occupies a large portion of most people's lives.

Yet many couples only discuss work in passing, often focusing on frustrations rather than understanding the bigger picture of what their partner does.

Showing curiosity about your partner's work communicates interest and respect for an important part of their life.

You don't need to fully understand every detail of their job.

But asking questions about their experiences, challenges, and achievements can strengthen connection.

It reinforces the idea that you care about what matters to them.

Ask your partner:

"What's something interesting that happened at work recently?"

How much do you really understand about what your partner experiences in their work life?

Hack 68
Maintain Individuality

A healthy relationship involves both **togetherness and individuality**.

While spending time together is important, maintaining personal interests and friendships outside the relationship is equally valuable.

Individual pursuits allow each partner to grow, recharge, and bring fresh energy back into the relationship.

When individuality is respected, partners avoid feelings of suffocation or dependency.

Instead, they create a balanced dynamic where both people feel free to be themselves.

Healthy relationships are strengthened when partners support each other's independence while remaining emotionally connected.

Encourage your partner to spend time doing something they enjoy independently this week.

Do you feel comfortable maintaining your own interests outside the relationship?

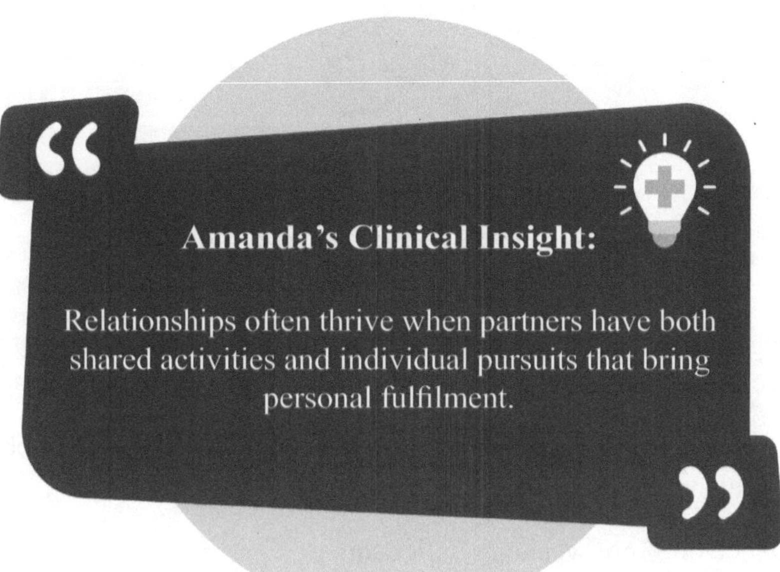
Amanda's Clinical Insight:
Relationships often thrive when partners have both shared activities and individual pursuits that bring personal fulfilment.

Hack 69
Support Independence

Supporting independence within a relationship demonstrates trust and confidence in the partnership.

It means encouraging your partner to maintain friendships, hobbies, and personal goals without feeling threatened by their independence.

Independence does not weaken relationships.

In fact, it often strengthens them.

When individuals feel supported in pursuing their own interests, they return to the relationship feeling energised and fulfilled.

This balance between independence and connection creates a dynamic where both partners feel respected and valued.

Ask your partner:

"Is there something you'd like more time or space to pursue?"

Do you see independence as a threat or a healthy part of a relationship?

Amanda's Tough Love Truth:

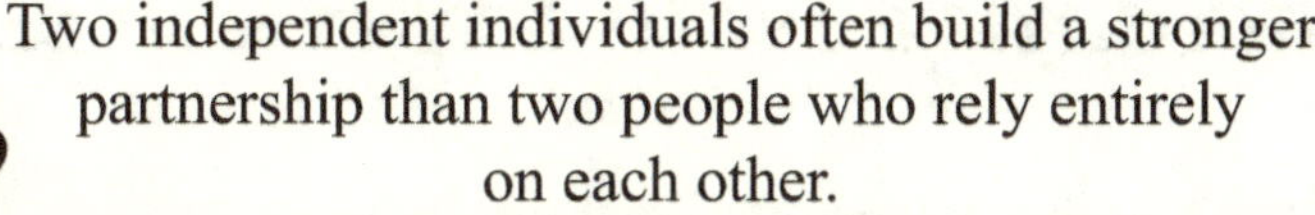

Two independent individuals often build a stronger partnership than two people who rely entirely on each other.

Hack 70
Encourage New Experiences

Trying new things together keeps relationships exciting.

Over time, routines can make life feel predictable. While routines offer comfort, too much predictability can lead to boredom.

Introducing new experiences can reignite curiosity and create memorable moments.

New experiences might include:

- visiting new places
- trying new activities
- exploring new hobbies
- attending events or workshops

These shared experiences strengthen the sense that the relationship is an adventure rather than just a routine.

Novelty stimulates the brain and can bring fresh energy into the relationship.

Plan one new experience to try together this month.

It doesn't have to be elaborate — even something small can create new memories.

When was the last time you and your partner tried something completely new together?

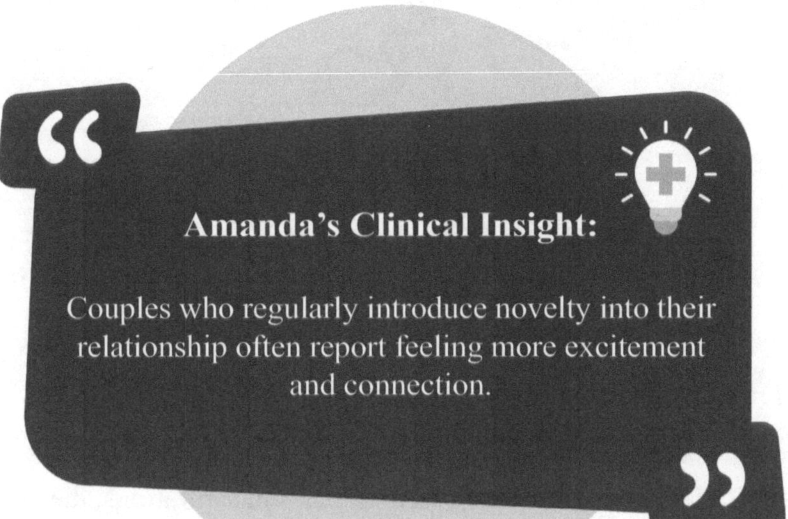
Amanda's Clinical Insight:
Couples who regularly introduce novelty into their relationship often report feeling more excitement and connection.

Hack 71
Create a Shared Vision for the Future

Healthy relationships are not just about enjoying the present moment. They are also about building a future together.

When couples talk about their long-term hopes and aspirations, they strengthen the sense that they are moving forward as a team.

A shared vision might include:

- travel plans
- family goals
- financial priorities
- lifestyle choices
- personal dreams

These conversations help couples align their expectations and feel excited about the future they are building together.

Without these discussions, partners may quietly begin moving in different directions without realizing it.

A shared vision provides both clarity and motivation.

Ask your partner:

"What's something you'd love for us to experience together in the next five years?"

Do you and your partner regularly talk about the future you want to create together?

Amanda's Tough Love Truth:

Couples who stop talking about the future together often start drifting apart in the present.

Hack 72
Reflect on the Relationship Regularly

Many people regularly reflect on their work, finances, and personal goals.

But surprisingly few couples take time to reflect on the health of their relationship.

Reflection helps couples notice what is working well and where improvements may be helpful.

These conversations allow both partners to stay emotionally aligned and avoid small frustrations building over time.

Reflection doesn't have to feel heavy or serious.

Sometimes it simply means asking:

"How are we doing lately?"

Healthy couples remain curious about the wellbeing of the relationship itself.

Set aside ten minutes this week to ask each other:

"What's one thing we've been doing well in our relationship recently?"

When was the last time you and your partner intentionally talked about the health of your relationship?

Hack 73
Acknowledge and Celebrate Change

Relationships evolve over time.

The people you are today are not exactly the same people you were when the relationship first began.

Life experiences, challenges, successes, and personal growth all shape who we become.

Healthy couples recognise and celebrate this evolution rather than resisting it.

They acknowledge how their partner has grown and express appreciation for the ways the relationship has developed.

Recognising change allows couples to honour the journey they have taken together.

Ask your partner:

"What is something you think we've both grown in since we first met?"

Do you take time to acknowledge how your relationship has evolved over time?

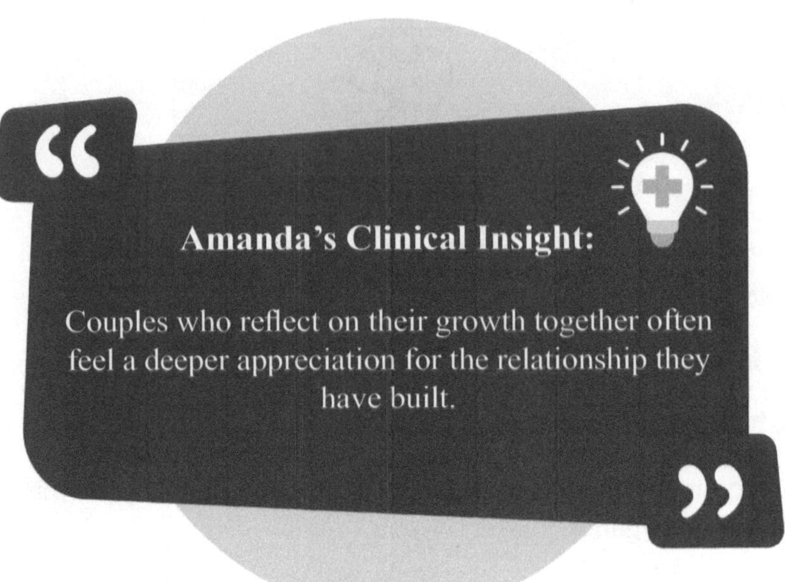
Amanda's Clinical Insight:
Couples who reflect on their growth together often feel a deeper appreciation for the relationship they have built.

Hack 74
Grow Through Challenges Together

Every relationship faces challenges.

Difficult periods may include career stress, financial pressure, health issues, family challenges, or unexpected life changes.

While these experiences can be stressful, they also offer opportunities for growth.

Couples who approach challenges as a team often emerge stronger.

Instead of blaming each other for difficulties, they focus on supporting one another through the experience.

Facing challenges together reinforces the sense that the relationship is a partnership built on resilience and trust.

During a challenging period, remind your partner:

“We’re in this together.”

How do you and your partner typically respond when life becomes difficult?

Amanda's Tough Love Truth:

Challenges don't break strong relationships.
Facing them alone does.

Hack 75
Expand Your Relationship Skills

Just as people invest in learning skills for their careers, relationships benefit from continued learning as well.

Communication, emotional awareness, and conflict resolution are skills that can be developed over time.

Healthy couples remain open to learning new strategies that help their relationship grow.

This might include:

- reading books about relationships
- attending workshops or seminars
- participating in counselling
- having meaningful conversations about personal growth

The willingness to learn together demonstrates commitment to the relationship's long-term health.

Choose one relationship skill you'd both like to improve and discuss how you can practice it together.

Are you open to continuing to learn new skills that strengthen your relationship?

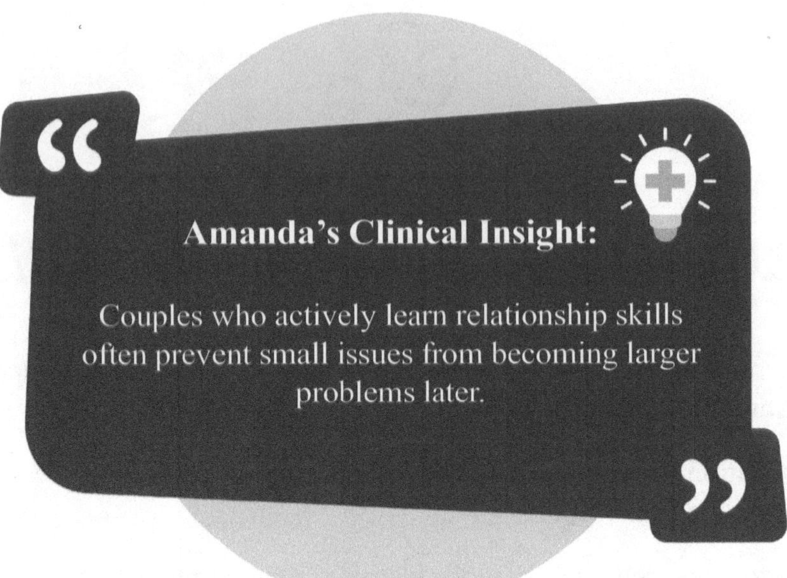
Amanda's Clinical Insight:
Couples who actively learn relationship skills often prevent small issues from becoming larger problems later.

Hack 76
Develop Emotional Intelligence Together

Emotional intelligence is the ability to recognise, understand, and manage emotions — both your own and your partner's.

In relationships, emotional intelligence allows partners to navigate difficult conversations with empathy rather than defensiveness.

It includes skills such as:

- recognising emotional triggers
- expressing feelings clearly
- responding with empathy
- managing emotional reactions during conflict

Couples who develop emotional intelligence together tend to communicate more effectively and resolve disagreements more constructively.

Instead of reacting impulsively, they learn to respond thoughtfully.

Over time, emotional intelligence becomes one of the strongest foundations for a resilient relationship.

During your next conversation about a difficult topic, pause and ask yourself:

"What emotion might my partner be experiencing right now?"

How well do you and your partner understand each other's emotional responses?

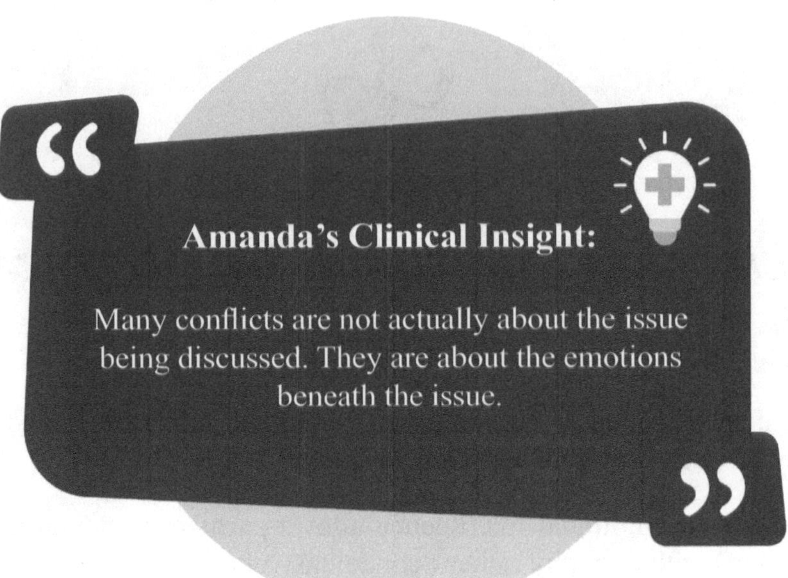
Amanda's Clinical Insight:
Many conflicts are not actually about the issue being discussed. They are about the emotions beneath the issue.

Hack 77
Invest in Mental Wellbeing Together

Mental wellbeing has a powerful influence on relationships.

When individuals are overwhelmed by stress, anxiety, or emotional fatigue, it becomes harder to communicate effectively and remain patient with each other.

Healthy couples recognise the importance of supporting each other's mental wellbeing.

This might include:

- encouraging healthy routines
- discussing emotional stress openly
- prioritising rest and self-care
- seeking professional support when needed

Investing in mental wellbeing strengthens both individuals and the relationship itself.

When both partners feel emotionally supported, the relationship becomes a source of stability rather than additional pressure.

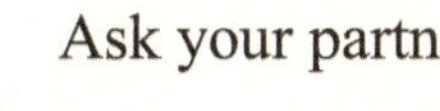

Ask your partner:

"What's one thing that helps you relax or recharge when life feels overwhelming?"

How do you and your partner support each other's emotional wellbeing?

Amanda's Tough Love Truth:

You cannot pour energy into your relationship if your own wellbeing is constantly depleted.

Hack 78
Explore Personal Development as a Couple

Personal growth becomes even more meaningful when couples explore it together.

Attending workshops, reading books, listening to podcasts, or participating in retreats can spark valuable conversations and shared learning experiences.

These experiences help couples develop new perspectives and strengthen their communication skills.

Exploring personal development together reinforces the idea that the relationship itself is something worth investing in.

It also creates opportunities to grow individually while strengthening the partnership.

Choose a book, podcast, or workshop about relationships or personal development and discuss it together.

When was the last time you intentionally invested in personal growth as a couple?

Hack 79
Encourage Lifelong Learning

Curiosity keeps relationships interesting.

Couples who continue learning throughout life often bring new ideas, experiences, and perspectives into the relationship.

Learning might involve:

- exploring new subjects
- attending courses
- developing new skills
- engaging with new ideas

When partners encourage each other's curiosity and learning, the relationship remains intellectually stimulating and engaging.

Learning also reinforces adaptability — an important trait for long-term relationships navigating life's many changes.

Ask your partner:

"Is there something new you'd love to learn in the next year?"

Do you and your partner encourage each other's curiosity and learning?

Hack 80
Maintain Curiosity About Each Other

Even after many years together, there is always more to learn about your partner.

People grow, change, and develop new interests throughout life.

Healthy couples remain curious about these changes rather than assuming they already know everything about each other.

Maintaining curiosity encourages meaningful conversations and deeper understanding.

It reminds partners that the relationship is a dynamic connection between two evolving individuals.

Curiosity keeps the relationship feeling fresh and engaging.

Ask your partner:

"What's something about you that has changed in the last few years?"

Do you still approach your partner with curiosity, or do you assume you already know everything about them?

Amanda's Tough Love Truth:

Relationships stay interesting when partners remain curious about each other.

Section 4 Exercise

The Future Vision Conversation

Strong couples regularly talk about where they are heading together.

This exercise helps you reconnect around shared goals and dreams.

How It Works

Discuss the following questions together.

- What would we like our life to look like in five years?
- What experiences would we love to have together?
- What personal goals can we support each other in achieving?

The Goal

When couples build a shared vision, they move from simply maintaining the relationship to **growing together intentionally**.

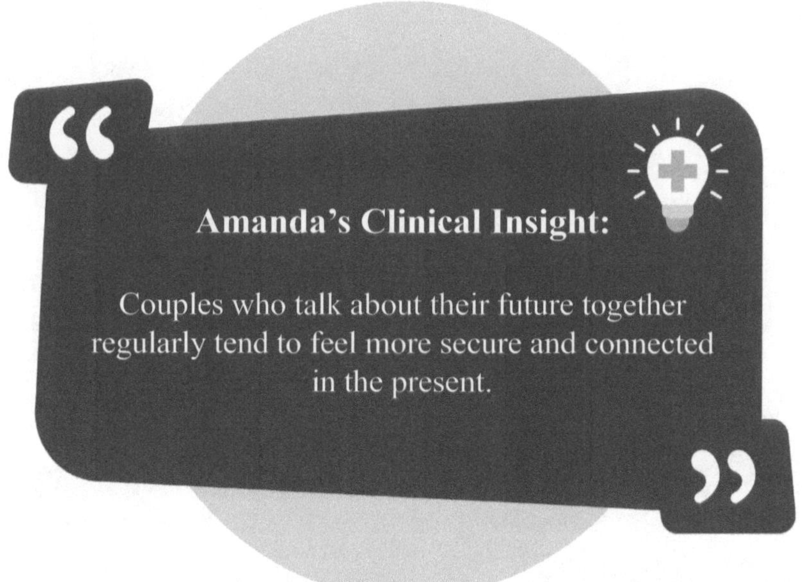

SECTION FIVE:

CREATING A LIFE TOGETHER

"A strong relationship isn't just about loving each other. It's about building a life you both enjoy living."

Why This Section Matters

A relationship is more than a series of conversations and responsibilities.

It is a shared life.

Over time, couples build routines, traditions, experiences, and memories that shape their partnership. These shared experiences create the emotional history that makes a relationship feel meaningful and unique.

However, when couples become overly focused on managing responsibilities, the relationship can start to feel like a series of tasks rather than a shared adventure.

Healthy relationships include joy, laughter, exploration, and moments of celebration.

Couples who intentionally create shared experiences often feel a stronger sense of partnership and appreciation for the life they are building together.

The hacks in this section encourage couples to prioritise shared experiences, celebrate milestones, and continue creating meaningful memories.

Because a relationship should not only be stable, it should also be fulfilling and enjoyable.

Amanda's Tough Love Truth:

A relationship shouldn't just survive life's responsibilities.
It should help you enjoy life more.

Why Shared Experiences Matter

At the beginning of a relationship, shared experiences come naturally.

Couples explore new places, try new activities, and create exciting memories together.

Over time, life often becomes more routine. Responsibilities increase, schedules become full, and the relationship can slowly shift from adventure to maintenance.

There is nothing wrong with routine. It provides stability and comfort.

But strong relationships also benefit from **shared experiences that bring energy, novelty, and joy back into the partnership**.

Shared experiences create stories.

They create laughter.

They create memories that remind couples why they enjoy being together.

The hacks in this section focus on building a life that both partners actively enjoy.

Amanda's Tough Love Truth:

A relationship that only revolves around responsibilities will eventually start to feel like work.
Shared joy keeps it alive.

Hack 81
Seek Shared Adventures

Adventure doesn't have to mean climbing mountains or travelling across the world.

It simply means stepping outside your usual routine together.

Adventure might look like:

- exploring a new part of your city
- trying a new restaurant
- taking a spontaneous day trip
- attending an event you've never experienced before

Shared adventures create memorable moments and strengthen emotional connection.

They remind couples that the relationship is not just about responsibilities, but about experiencing life together.

Plan one small adventure together this month — something new for both of you.

When was the last time you and your partner tried something completely new together?

Hack 82
Cultivate Shared Interests

Shared interests provide opportunities for couples to spend enjoyable time together.

These interests might include:

- cooking
- sports
- travel
- creative hobbies
- outdoor activities

You don't have to share every interest, but finding activities that both partners genuinely enjoy strengthens the sense of partnership.

Shared hobbies create regular opportunities for connection and conversation.

They also help couples maintain a sense of fun within the relationship.

Ask your partner:

"What's an activity you think we would both enjoy trying together?"

Do you and your partner have hobbies or interests you enjoy sharing?

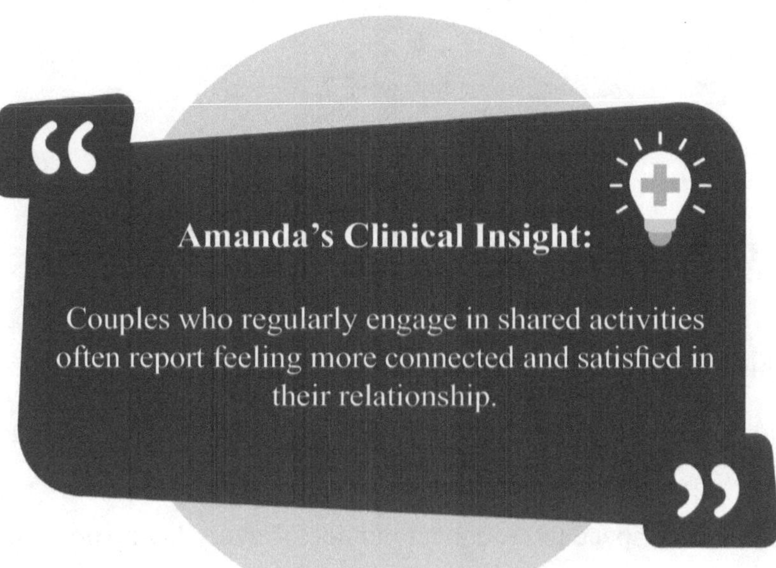
Amanda's Clinical Insight:
Couples who regularly engage in shared activities often report feeling more connected and satisfied in their relationship.

Hack 83
Schedule Regular Date Nights

Date nights are not just for new relationships.

In fact, long-term relationships often benefit the most from intentional time together.

Date nights create space to reconnect outside of everyday responsibilities.

They allow couples to talk, laugh, and enjoy each other's company without distractions.

Research consistently shows that couples who prioritise regular time together experience stronger emotional connection.

Date nights do not need to be elaborate or expensive.

What matters most is the intention behind them.

Schedule one date night in the next two weeks and protect that time from interruptions.

How often do you and your partner intentionally create time just for the two of you?

Amanda's Tough Love Truth:

If your relationship only gets the time that's left over after everything else, it will eventually start to feel neglected.

Hack 84
Create Rituals Together

Rituals are small traditions that couples create and repeat over time.

They provide comfort, predictability, and emotional connection.

Rituals might include:

- Sunday morning coffee together
- a regular evening walk
- cooking dinner together on certain nights
- celebrating anniversaries in a special way

These rituals become meaningful anchors within the relationship.

They remind couples to pause and reconnect regularly.

Over time, these traditions become cherished parts of the relationship story.

Create one simple weekly ritual that you both look forward to.

What rituals currently exist in your relationship?

Hack 85
Maintain a Spirit of Adventure

Adventure doesn't disappear with time.

It simply needs to be nurtured intentionally.

Maintaining a spirit of adventure means staying open to new experiences and continuing to explore life together.

It might involve:

- spontaneous plans
- learning new skills together
- travelling somewhere new
- stepping outside comfort zones

Adventure stimulates curiosity and creates shared excitement.

Couples who maintain a sense of adventure often feel their relationship remains vibrant and energising.

Ask your partner:

"What's something adventurous you'd love for us to try together?"

Does your relationship still feel exciting and exploratory?

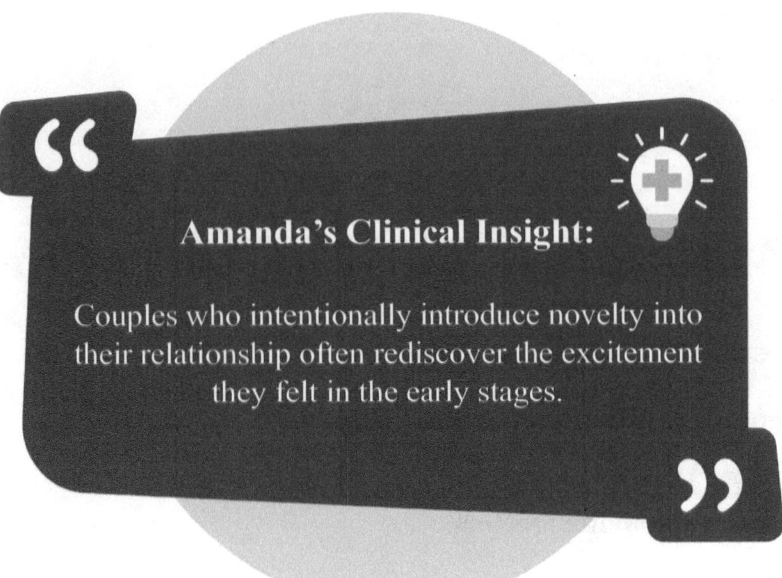
Amanda's Clinical Insight:
Couples who intentionally introduce novelty into their relationship often rediscover the excitement they felt in the early stages.

Hack 86
Document Adventures Together

Memories are one of the most meaningful parts of a relationship.

The trips you've taken, the unexpected moments, the stories you still laugh about years later. These shared experiences become part of the relationship's identity.

Taking the time to document adventures together helps preserve those memories.

This might include:

- taking photos during trips
- keeping a travel journal
- creating a shared photo album
- revisiting favourite memories together

Looking back on these experiences reminds couples of the journey they have taken together and reinforces the emotional connection they have built.

Memories are powerful anchors in long-term relationships.

Choose one recent photo or memory and reminisce about it together tonight.

What is one shared memory that always makes you smile when you think about it?

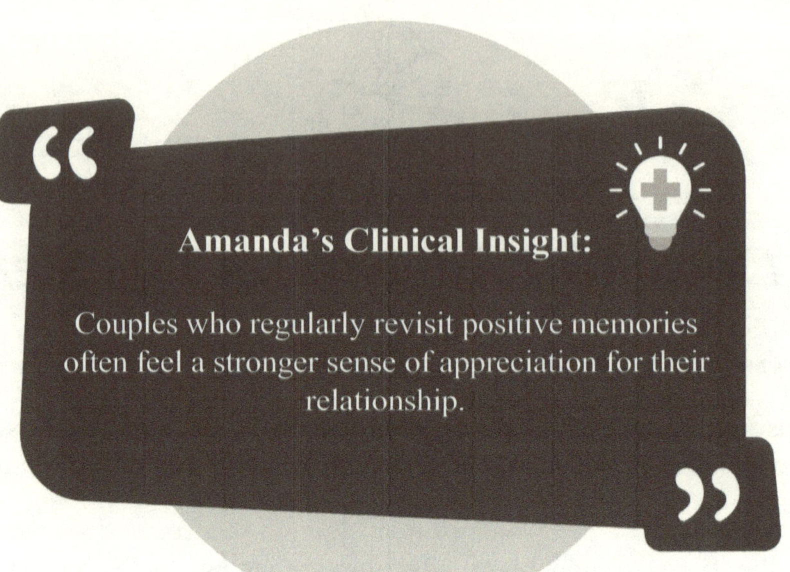
Amanda's Clinical Insight:
Couples who regularly revisit positive memories often feel a stronger sense of appreciation for their relationship.

Hack 87
Create a Bucket List Together

A bucket list isn't just about big dreams. It's about creating a shared sense of possibility.

When couples talk about experiences they would love to have together, it brings excitement and anticipation into the relationship.

Your bucket list might include:

- travelling to specific places
- learning new skills together
- attending special events
- achieving personal goals as a team

These conversations help couples feel like they are building something meaningful together.

Even small goals can bring joy when they are shared.

Sit down together and write a list of **five experiences you'd love to share in the next few years.**

What is one experience you would love to have together that you haven't planned yet?

Amanda's Tough Love Truth:

Couples who stop dreaming together often stop growing together.

Hack 88
Plan Surprises for Each Other

Surprises add a sense of excitement and thoughtfulness to relationships.

They don't need to be extravagant. Often the most meaningful surprises are small gestures that show consideration and care.

Examples might include:

- leaving a thoughtful note
- planning an unexpected outing
- cooking your partner's favourite meal
- organising a spontaneous date

Surprises communicate that you are thinking about your partner and want to make them feel special.

Even small gestures can create moments of joy and appreciation.

Plan a small surprise for your partner this week — something that shows you were thinking about them.

When was the last time you did something unexpected to make your partner smile?

Hack 89
Celebrate Culture and Traditions

Every person brings their own cultural background, traditions, and family experiences into a relationship.

Honouring these traditions helps partners feel respected and understood.

It might include celebrating holidays, maintaining meaningful family customs, or exploring each other's cultural heritage.

These traditions can enrich the relationship and create shared experiences that feel meaningful and memorable.

Celebrating traditions together strengthens the sense of belonging within the relationship.

Talk about one tradition from your family that you would love to continue or share with your partner.

What traditions or cultural experiences have shaped who you are today?

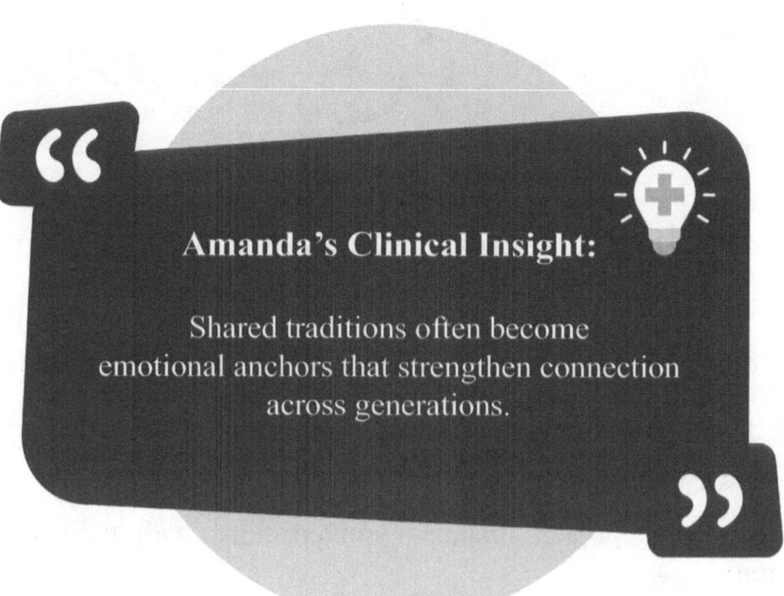
Amanda's Clinical Insight:
Shared traditions often become emotional anchors that strengthen connection across generations.

Hack 90
Talk Openly About Finances

Money is one of the most common sources of tension in relationships.

Different financial habits, expectations, and attitudes toward spending can create conflict if they are not discussed openly.

Healthy couples approach financial conversations with transparency and cooperation.

This might include discussing:

- spending habits
- savings goals
- financial responsibilities
- long-term financial plans

Open financial communication helps couples avoid misunderstandings and ensures both partners feel informed and involved.

Financial conversations may feel uncomfortable at first, but they are essential for building trust and stability.

Schedule a relaxed conversation about financial goals and priorities for the coming year.

Do you and your partner feel comfortable discussing finances openly?

Amanda's Tough Love Truth:

Avoiding financial conversations doesn't prevent conflict — it usually delays it.

Hack 91
Maintain a Shared Calendar

Life can become busy very quickly.

Work commitments, social activities, family responsibilities, and personal schedules can easily become overwhelming if partners are not aligned.

A shared calendar helps couples stay organised and informed about each other's schedules.

It reduces misunderstandings and prevents situations where one partner feels overlooked or left out of important plans.

Whether you use a digital calendar or a simple planner, having visibility into each other's commitments helps partners coordinate their time and maintain balance.

More importantly, it helps couples protect time for their relationship.

Set up a shared calendar and include important events, commitments, and planned time together.

How well do you and your partner understand each other's weekly schedules?

Hack 92
Share Responsibilities Fairly

One of the most common sources of frustration in relationships is an imbalance in responsibilities.

When one partner feels they are carrying a disproportionate share of household or family responsibilities, resentment can slowly build.

Healthy couples regularly communicate about responsibilities and adjust them as life circumstances change.

Fairness does not necessarily mean everything is divided exactly equally. It means both partners feel the division of responsibilities is reasonable and supportive.

Open conversations about responsibilities help prevent misunderstandings and ensure both partners feel valued.

Discuss one area of responsibility in your household and explore whether it feels balanced for both of you.

Do both partners feel the responsibilities in the relationship are shared fairly?

Amanda's Tough Love Truth:

Resentment often grows quietly when responsibilities feel one-sided.

Hack 93
Make Decisions Together

Major decisions in life often affect both partners.

Whether it involves career changes, financial commitments, family planning, or lifestyle choices, discussing decisions together reinforces the sense of partnership.

Healthy couples recognise that decision-making is a shared process.

This does not mean both partners must agree on every detail, but it does mean that each person's perspective is considered and respected.

Collaborative decision-making strengthens trust and ensures both partners feel included in the direction of the relationship.

Before making an important decision, ask your partner:

"How do you feel about this?"

Do both partners feel heard when important decisions are being made?

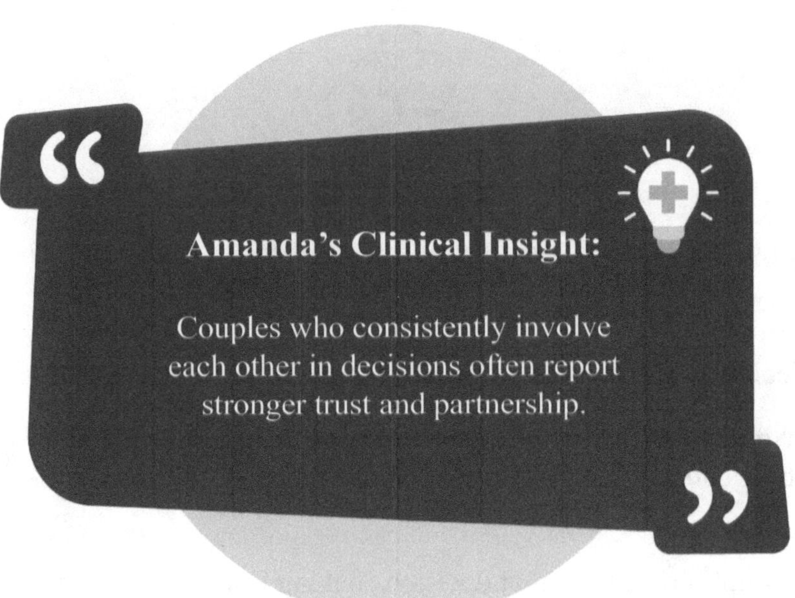
Amanda's Clinical Insight:
Couples who consistently involve each other in decisions often report stronger trust and partnership.

Hack 94
Create a Mutual Support Network

Relationships thrive when couples feel supported not only by each other, but also by a broader community.

Friends, family members, mentors, and supportive social connections can provide encouragement, perspective, and companionship.

A healthy support network can help couples navigate life's challenges and celebrate important milestones together.

Maintaining strong social connections also helps prevent the relationship from becoming isolated or overly dependent on a single source of emotional support.

Community strengthens resilience.

Reach out to a couple or friend you enjoy spending time with and plan a shared activity.

Who are the supportive people in your lives that strengthen your relationship?

Hack 95
Volunteer Together

Helping others can be an incredibly meaningful shared experience.

Volunteering together allows couples to contribute to something larger than themselves while strengthening their sense of partnership.

Whether it involves community projects, charity events, mentoring programs, or environmental initiatives, volunteering can create a shared sense of purpose.

Research shows that couples who engage in meaningful activities together often feel a deeper sense of connection and fulfilment.

Acts of service also reinforce shared values and compassion.

Identify one organisation or cause you both care about and explore opportunities to contribute together.

What values do you and your partner share that could be expressed through helping others?

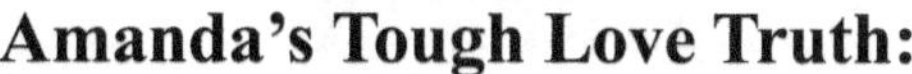

Amanda's Tough Love Truth:

Shared purpose often strengthens relationships far more than shared convenience.

Hack 96
Adopt Shared Projects

Shared projects can bring couples closer together by creating opportunities for teamwork and collaboration.

A project doesn't need to be complicated. It simply needs to be something both partners care about and can contribute to.

Examples might include:

- renovating part of your home
- starting a garden
- planning a trip together
- working on a creative project
- organising a family event

Shared projects give couples a sense of accomplishment and reinforce the idea that they are building something meaningful together.

Working toward a common goal strengthens cooperation and communication.

Choose one small project you could work on together over the next few weeks.

What is something you and your partner could create or accomplish together?

Hack 97
Plan the Future Together

Planning the future as a couple reinforces the idea that you are building a life side by side.

Conversations about the future might include topics such as:

- travel dreams
- career aspirations
- family plans
- lifestyle choices
- personal goals

These discussions help partners align their expectations and ensure they are moving in the same direction.

When couples actively plan their future together, the relationship feels purposeful and intentional.

Set aside time to discuss one goal you would both like to achieve together within the next few years.

How often do you and your partner talk about the future you want to create together?

Amanda's Tough Love Truth:

A shared future doesn't happen automatically. It's built through intentional conversations and decisions.

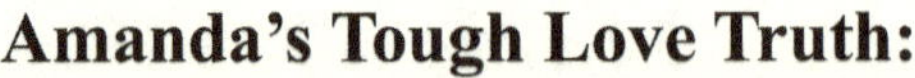

Hack 98
Celebrate Important Milestones

Milestones deserve recognition.

Anniversaries, career achievements, personal accomplishments, and life transitions all represent meaningful moments in a couple's journey together.

Celebrating these milestones helps partners pause and appreciate how far they have come.

It also creates positive memories that strengthen emotional connection.

Even simple celebrations can reinforce appreciation and gratitude within the relationship.

Plan a meaningful way to celebrate your next anniversary or important milestone together.

How do you and your partner currently celebrate significant moments in your lives?

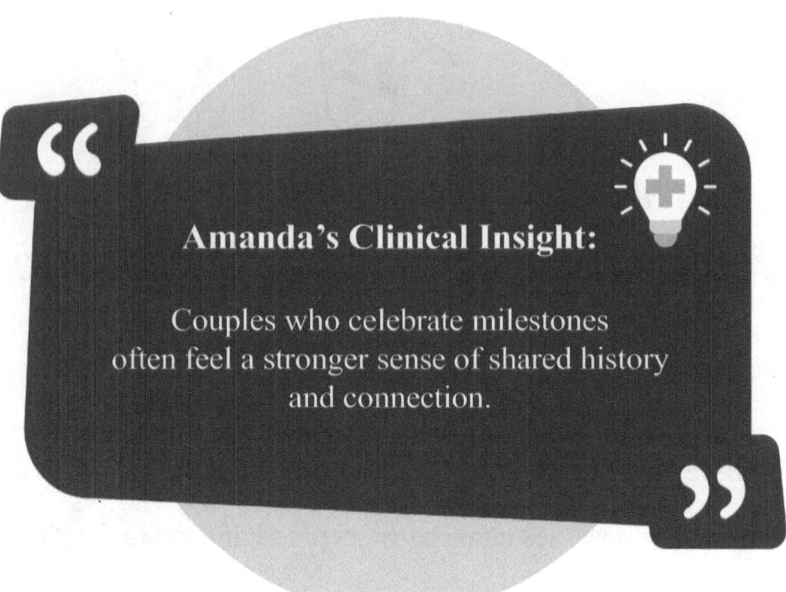
Amanda's Clinical Insight:
Couples who celebrate milestones often feel a stronger sense of shared history and connection.

Hack 99
Build a Shared Life Vision

A relationship becomes even more meaningful when partners share a vision for the life they want to create together.

A shared life vision includes:

• the values you want to live by
• the experiences you want to have
• the kind of environment you want to build together

Discussing this vision allows couples to align their priorities and make decisions that support their shared goals.

It turns the relationship into something more than a partnership of convenience.

It becomes a **collaborative life journey**.

Ask each other:

"What kind of life do we want to look back on together one day?"

Do you and your partner have a clear vision of the life you want to build together?

Hack 100
Prioritise Each Other's Happiness

At the heart of every strong relationship is a simple commitment:

Caring about each other's wellbeing.

This does not mean sacrificing your own needs or constantly trying to please your partner.

It means recognising that your partner's happiness matters to you.

Healthy couples support each other, celebrate each other's successes, and look for ways to contribute positively to each other's lives.

When both partners prioritise the wellbeing of the other, the relationship becomes a place of encouragement, trust, and joy.

Ask your partner today:

"What's one thing I could do this week that would make your life a little easier or happier?"

How do you and your partner contribute to each other's happiness?

Amanda's Tough Love Truth:

Strong relationships are built when two people consistently choose to care about each other's wellbeing.

Section 5 Exercise

The Relationship Check-In Ritual

This exercise is designed to keep your relationship healthy long-term.

Think of it as a regular relationship maintenance check.

How It Works

Once a week, ask each other the following three questions.

1. What is something you appreciated about me this week?
2. Is there anything we should adjust or improve in our relationship right now?
3. What is something you are looking forward to together this week?

The Goal

This ritual keeps communication open and prevents small frustrations from building into larger issues.

Bonus Section

20 Quick Relationship Boosters

Sometimes the smallest actions can have the biggest impact in a relationship.

Here are twenty simple reminders that can instantly strengthen connection when practiced consistently.

101. Kiss hello and goodbye every day.
102. Say "thank you" more often than you think necessary.
103. Turn your phone face down when your partner is speaking.
104. Never underestimate the power of a genuine hug.
105. Tell your partner what you admire about them.
106. Laugh about small mistakes instead of criticising them.
107. Check in with your partner before assuming how they feel.
108. Protect time together as fiercely as you protect work commitments.
109. Celebrate effort, not just outcomes.
110. Ask your partner how you can support them today.
111. Leave a thoughtful message or note when they least expect it.
112. Remember that kindness during stressful moments matters most.
113. Share one thing you're grateful for about your partner every day.

114. Try something new together at least once a month.
115. Encourage your partner's dreams, even when they feel uncertain.
116. Hold hands during walks or quiet moments together.
117. Apologise quickly when you realise you're wrong.
118. Speak about your partner with respect, even when they aren't present.
119. Protect your relationship from unnecessary outside negativity.
120. Keep choosing each other, even on the ordinary days.

Amanda's Tough Love Truth:

Relationships rarely fail because of one big mistake. More often, they weaken when couples stop practicing the small habits that keep connection strong.

A Final Word

If you've made it this far, I want to take a moment to acknowledge something important.

You care about your relationship.

That might sound obvious, but in reality many people move through life without ever pausing to reflect on how their relationships are functioning or what they could do to strengthen them.

Simply opening this book and exploring these ideas shows a willingness to invest in something that truly matters.

Over the years I've worked with thousands of individuals and couples navigating the joys and challenges of relationships. I've seen relationships struggling under the weight of misunderstanding, stress, and disconnection. I've also seen relationships flourish when couples decide to approach their partnership with curiosity, compassion, and commitment.

One of the most powerful lessons I've learned through this work is that strong relationships are not built through perfection.

They are built through intention.

Small actions.
Thoughtful conversations.
Moments of kindness.
Choosing to listen rather than react.
Choosing to reconnect even after difficult moments.

These choices may seem small at the time, but over months and years they shape the emotional foundation of a relationship.

Relationships are living, evolving partnerships between two people who are constantly growing and changing. That means the work of nurturing a relationship is never truly "finished."

And that's not a bad thing.

In fact, it's one of the most meaningful parts of sharing life with another person.

When both partners remain willing to learn, communicate openly, and invest in the connection, relationships can become a source of deep support, joy, and personal growth.

If even a handful of the hacks in this book help you communicate more clearly, appreciate each other more often, or reconnect in meaningful ways, then the purpose of this book has been fulfilled.

Remember that relationships are not strengthened through occasional grand gestures.

They are strengthened through consistent care.

So keep choosing to listen.
Keep choosing kindness.
Keep choosing curiosity.
And most importantly, keep choosing each other.

Because when two people continue investing in their relationship, the results can be extraordinary.

With warmth,

Amanda

The 30-Day Relationship Reset

Reading about relationships is helpful.

Practicing new relationship habits is where real change happens.

If you're ready to take the ideas in this book one step further, I invite you to try something simple but powerful: a **30-Day Relationship Reset**.

For the next 30 days, choose **one relationship hack each day** from this book and intentionally practice it with your partner.

That's it.

No complicated systems.
No overwhelming changes.

Just small, consistent actions.

Over the course of a month, those small actions can begin to shift the tone of your relationship in meaningful ways.

How It Works

1. Choose one hack each day from the book.
2. Discuss it briefly with your partner.
3. Practice the micro action suggested in the hack.
4. Reflect together at the end of the day.

You may notice that some hacks feel natural, while others require more effort. That's completely normal.

Relationships grow when we practice new behaviours consistently.

The Goal

The goal of the 30-Day Relationship Reset isn't perfection.

It's awareness.

It's about intentionally paying attention to your relationship again.

Many couples discover that even small shifts — listening more carefully, expressing appreciation more often, or setting aside intentional time together — can dramatically improve connection.

Amanda's Tough Love Truth:

Relationships rarely improve because people hope things will get better.
They improve because people decide to invest in them.

A Simple Reflection

At the end of the 30 days, ask each other:

- What changes did we notice in our relationship?
- Which hacks had the biggest impact?
- What habits would we like to continue practicing?

You might be surprised by how much can shift in just one month.

Keep the Momentum Going

If you've completed the 30-Day Relationship Reset, congratulations. You've already made an investment in your relationship that many couples never take the time to make.

If you'd like ongoing tools and strategies to continue strengthening your relationship, I invite you to explore the **Relationship Recharge Membership**, where we dive deeper into many of the concepts introduced in this book.

Because strong relationships are not built overnight.

They are built through small, intentional actions practiced over time.

And every investment you make in your relationship today helps create the partnership you want tomorrow.

Ready for a Relationship Reset?

Sometimes couples need more than tips. They need a focused space to reconnect, rebuild trust, and learn new relationship skills together.

That's why I also offer **Relationship Intensives**.

These intensives are designed for couples who want to:

- improve communication
- repair trust
- strengthen emotional intimacy
- reconnect after difficult periods
- future-proof their relationship

Instead of spending months in traditional therapy, intensives allow couples to work deeply on their relationship over a concentrated period of time.

Couples leave with clarity, practical tools, and a renewed sense of partnership.

If you're ready to invest in the future of your relationship, I invite you to explore the intensive programs.

👉 Learn more at: **www.amandalambros.com**

About Amanda Lambros

Amanda Lambros is a relationship therapist, clinical supervisor, and international speaker with more than two decades of experience helping individuals and couples build stronger relationships.

She is known for her practical, no-nonsense approach to relationships and her ability to translate complex psychological concepts into strategies people can actually use in their daily lives.

Amanda works with couples, professionals, and leaders who want to strengthen their relationships, improve communication, and invest in their emotional wellbeing.

Her work focuses on what she calls **Mental Wealth** — the idea that investing in emotional wellbeing and relationships creates lasting personal and professional success.

Amanda is also the creator of the **Relationship Recharge Membership**, a community designed to help couples continuously strengthen their relationship through practical tools and insights.

When she's not working with clients or speaking internationally, Amanda enjoys travelling, spending time with her family, and occasionally attempting hobbies that her husband enjoys far more than she does.

Learn more at:
www.amandalambros.com

NOT QUITE READY TO SAY GOODBYE?

If you've enjoyed spending time in these pages, the good news is this isn't where it ends. Amanda offers a range of ways to support you beyond the book, from relationship coaching to wellbeing programs and more.

Take a look at what's next on the following pages, or head to www.amandalambros.com to keep the momentum going. You'll also find her online, sharing tips, tools, and a little behind-the-scenes reality.

www.amandalambros.com

Are You Ready to Strengthen Your Relationship for the Long Term?

Most people don't set out to have a disconnected relationship.
It just… happens.

Life gets busy. Communication slips. Small things go unsaid. And before you know it, you're living alongside each other instead of truly connecting.

If you've read this book and found yourself thinking,
"We could be better than this…"
then you're already on the right track.

The next step is consistency.

That's exactly what the Relationship Recharge Membership is designed for.

What You'll Experience Inside

Month 1: Rebuilding Connection
Month 2: Love Languages & Lasting Connection
Month 3: Communication that Connects
Month 4: Emotional Safety & Vulnerability
Month 5: Managing Financial Stress Together
Month 6: Rekindling Romance & Fun
Month 7: Shared Responsibilities & Teamwork
Month 8: Boundaries, Space and Self Care
Month 9: Rebuilding After Conflict
Month 10: Sex, Intimacy & Real Connection
Month 11: Gratitude & Generosity
Month 12: Creating Your Relationship Rhythm

To find out more about the program, please visit:
https://relationship-recharge.com/

Looking for the Perfect Gift for a Couple You Care About?

We all want to give gifts that mean something. Something thoughtful, something useful, something that actually makes a difference. And while flowers fade and gadgets get forgotten, a stronger, more connected relationship is a gift that lasts.

The Relationship Recharge Membership offers something far more meaningful than a traditional present. Whether it's for a couple celebrating an engagement or wedding, marking an anniversary, adjusting to life as new parents, or simply friends you care about deeply, this is a gift that supports their relationship in a lasting and practical way.

Most couples don't lack love. They lack time, tools, and guidance. This gift gently gives them all three. Instead of guessing what might help, you're offering practical strategies to improve communication, tools to navigate challenges, and simple ways to reconnect and stay connected. It's not about fixing anything. It's about strengthening what's already there.

Unlike a one-off experience, this is something they can return to again and again. Each month, they'll receive guidance and support to help them stay connected through busy seasons, handle conflict with more ease, build emotional safety and trust, and keep their relationship a priority rather than an afterthought. It's a gift that grows with them over time.

You can choose to gift the membership as a full 12-month experience, as a thoughtful surprise for a special occasion, or even as a simple gesture to say "I'm thinking of you." Sometimes the most meaningful gifts aren't things, they're experiences that bring people closer together.

To gift the Relationship Recharge Membership, or to find out more, visit www relationship-recharge.com.

Because the best gift you can give a couple is the opportunity to keep choosing each other.

Not All Relationship Coaches Are Created Equal

Relationships today are more complex than ever. The way we communicate, connect, and navigate life together has evolved, yet many of the approaches people rely on remain outdated, surface-level, or ineffective in real-world situations. Building a strong, lasting relationship now requires more than intention. It requires the ability to learn, unlearn, and relearn how we show up, both individually and as a couple.

Amanda Lambros works with a limited number of individuals and couples who are ready to move beyond repeated patterns and create meaningful, lasting change. Her work is grounded in over two decades of experience, combining evidence-based practice with deep insight into human behaviour. This is not about quick fixes or generic advice. It is for those who are prepared to take responsibility, engage honestly, and invest in doing the work required to build a relationship that is not only functional, but deeply connected and fulfilling.

This level of work is not for everyone. It is for those who are ready to move past surface conversations and step into a more intentional, accountable, and growth-oriented way of relating. It is not about avoiding conflict or maintaining appearances. It is about developing the emotional intelligence, communication skills, and awareness needed to create a relationship that can truly thrive.

If there is one message to take from this book, it is this: exceptional relationships are not left to chance, they are built with intention, commitment, and the right support.

To enquire about working with Amanda, please visit **www.amandalambros.com** or email **info@amandalambros.com**.

Would You Like to Interview Amanda Lambros?

With over two decades of experience as a relationship therapist, sexologist, and mental wellbeing expert, Amanda Lambros is a trusted voice across media in Australia and internationally. She is highly experienced across all formats, from live television and radio to print features, panel discussions, and in-depth interviews. Amanda brings a balance of professional insight, real-world experience, and relatable delivery, making complex topics accessible, engaging, and genuinely useful for a wide range of audiences.

Amanda speaks with authority on relationships, communication, intimacy, mental health, emotional resilience, self-care, and the evolving complexities of modern relationships. She is known for translating clinical knowledge into practical, everyday strategies that audiences can immediately apply in their lives.

Signature Talking Points Include:

- The hidden reasons couples disconnect and how to reconnect
- Why communication breaks down and what actually works instead
- Redefining intimacy and what it really means to be "good in bed"
- The impact of mental load and emotional burnout on relationships
- Navigating modern relationships, from dating to long-term commitment
- Building emotional resilience and sustainable self-care
- How to create strong relationships in high-pressure, high-performance lives

Whether you are looking for an expert guest for an article, a media interview, or commentary for a feature, Amanda brings both depth and warmth to every conversation.

If you would like to interview Amanda or explore media opportunities in relation to this book or her work more broadly, please visit **www.amandalambros.com** or email **info@amandalambros.com**.

Looking for a Podcast Guest Who Brings Insight and Real Conversation?

If you're looking for a podcast guest who goes beyond surface-level advice and brings honest, insightful, and engaging conversation, Amanda Lambros is a natural fit.

With over 20 years of experience working with individuals and couples, Amanda offers a unique blend of clinical expertise and real-world perspective. She speaks openly about relationships, intimacy, mental health, and the realities of modern life, in a way t hat feels relatable, practical, and refreshingly human.

Amanda is comfortable across both structured interviews and free-flowing conversations, making her an easy and engaging guest for a wide range of podcast styles. Whether your audience is focused on relationships, personal development, leadership, or wellbeing, she brings valuable insights that resonate.

If you're looking to create a conversation your audience will connect with and remember, Amanda would love to join you.

To enquire about podcast interviews or availability, visit **www.amandalambros.com** or email **info@amandalambros.com**.

www.ingramcontent.com/pod-product-compliance
Lightning Source LLC
LaVergne TN
LVHW091037080826
845145LV00002B/530

* 9 7 8 1 9 2 3 2 3 7 0 0 1 *